P9-DWJ-220

Coping with
Sudden Infant
Death

Coping with Sudden Infant Death

John DeFrain
The University of Nebraska
Jacque Taylor
Office on Domestic Violence,
Riverton, Wyoming
Linda Ernst
University of Minnesota
and St. Olaf College

LexingtonBooks
D.C. Heath and Company
Lexington, Massachusetts
Toronto

Library of Congress Cataloging in Publication Data

DeFrain, John D.
  Coping with sudden infant death.

  Includes index.
  1. Sudden death in infants—Psychological aspects. 2. Bereavement—
Psychological aspects. 3. Parent and child. 4. Mental health surveys—United
States. I. Taylor, Jacque. II. Ernst, Linda. III. Title.
RJ59.D43   155.9'37   81-48626
  ISBN 0-669-05453-4 Casebound
  ISBN 0-669-05583-2 Paperbound

Copyright © 1982 by D.C. Heath and Company

Sixth printing, January 1986

Published simultaneously in Canada

Printed in the United States of America on acid-free paper

International Standard Book Number: 0-669-05453-4 Casebound

International Standard Book Number: 0-669-05583-2 Paperbound

Library of Congress Catalog Card Number: 81-48626

List of Figures

Acknowledgments

There is nothing new under the sun.—Ecclesiastes, 1:9

This we sincerely believe. The book you are about to read is not new or revolutionary. Rather, it is a small step ahead in the human search for understanding the nature and meaning of death—one small step, based on the lives and experiences of many people. If the reader finds it in any way helpful, we are gratified in our work, and thankful to the literally hundreds of people who have contributed immeasurably to it.

We would like to mention just of few of these good folks: John Woodward, Ph.D., associate dean of the College of Home Economics at the University of Nebraska-Lincoln, who decided research on families who experience sudden, unexplained infant death would be invaluable, and wrote a grant proposal; the Agricultural Experiment Station of the Institute of Agriculture and Natural Resources (IANR) at the University of Nebraska-Lincoln, which funded Dr. Woodward's proposal for a five-year study of families in crisis. Administrators in the IANR included Martin Massengale, Ph.D. (now chancellor of the University of Nebraska-Lincoln), Howard Ottoson, Ph.D., Robert Kleis, Ph.D., and Roy Arnold, Ph.D.; Nick Stinnett, Ph.D., chairman of the Department of Human Development and the Family; Hazel Anthony, Ed.D., dean of the College of Home Economics; Charlotte Jackson and Virginia Woodward, secretaries in Human Development and the Family; and Anne Parkhurst, M.S., statistical consultant in the Biometrics and Information Processing Center, University of Nebraska-Lincoln; Robert Grant, M.D., head of the Division of Maternal and Child Health of the Nebraska Department of Health, and Lorene Wood, R.N., who worked with us in finding SIDS families and convincing the families that the research had merit; William H. Marshall, Ph.D., University of Wisconsin-Madison, Charlene Gray, D.S.W., Catholic University of America, and Alan Fisher, M.D., a Lincoln physician, for carefully critiquing the manuscript; the anonymous benefactor who read of our early research in *Psychology Today* and gave us a financial and psychological boost through his Omaha investment and banking advisor, Piper, Jaffray and Hopwood; Margaret Zusky, editor, and the staff of Lexington Books, whose sensitivity and caring have made our work together so satisfying; our own families who appreciate the importance of our labors; the SIDS parents themselves who so unquestioningly gave of their time and their spirit.

To all of these people, a warm and heartfelt thank you.

1 Introduction

When a baby dies, suddenly, unexpectedly, and for no apparent reason, a unique crisis occurs in the family. The effect this crisis has on individual families manifests itself in many different ways.

For five years we have been conducting research on these families and have asked people across the United States, "What have you gone through since your baby died?" Replies came from eighty localities in twenty states in every corner of the nation; from cities, large and small; from rural communities and farms. Mothers and fathers who responded to our query were black and white, Chicano, Native American, Oriental. They were rich, poor, middle class. They represented many religious faiths. Some had graduate degrees, some graduated from the eighth grade. They were homemakers, bankers, professors, clerks, teachers, electricians, farmers. But the one point that became glaringly apparent, and the one factor they held in common, was their great need to share the experience of losing a baby to Sudden Infant Death Syndrome (SIDS). Here is but one mother's story, just as she told it to us:

> In the beginning I lost all sense of being. The second day after the funeral, I went out and tried to dig up her grave. I thought I could see her in her walker or hear her cry. I stayed up all of the day and night checking the other kids. I'd leave them several times a week and go to the cemetery and sit by her grave all afternoon. At the time I was four months pregnant. After my little boy was born, my husband and I took turns with four-hour shifts, watching the baby for several weeks. Then I would dress him in her clothes, until one day I put her shoes on him and I had to get my oldest child to take them off.

> I wouldn't allow her to be put in a casket until the day of the funeral. We had taken pictures of her at the funeral home but my husband wouldn't allow me to look at them. But they seemed to be some sort of a help. I can't really explain in words how they helped me. I never had but one other picture of her and it was when she was a newborn. The best I can explain this was just being able to look at her, it seemed she wasn't so far away. The pictures from the funeral home were not taken of her in a casket and she looked as though she was asleep.

> I still have periods of fear of losing the other children. Right after my baby died, my niece, four years old, drowned. Then my father was shot and killed. I lost all sense of reality. My husband started drinking and I hated

1

him. I couldn't sleep. If I did I had dreams about bugs eating her, or I'd dream of the funeral. Somewhere in the back of my mind I decided if I could just stop loving the kids, my husband, and parents, I could never be hurt by anyone or anything.

I knew I needed counseling, but my mom and husband were totally against anything like that. It was only for crazy people. But I finally went to one doctor for almost a year, and I lived in my grief and could talk to him, and am thankful to God he told me what a selfish mother I was being. Oh, I hated him at the time, but he is the only one who really helped me out of the loneliness, because I'd shut myself off from any feeling relationships.

My stepfather made some harsh statements; some people thought we were really to blame. When it happened we were visiting my mother and the baby was in bed with us; my husband had been drinking and thought he had suffocated her. My husband wanted to send the pictures we had taken of her to his mother. I hated him and blamed him. She had awoken for a two o'clock feeding and we played and she laughed and cooed, and at six o'clock she was dead. My husband never said so in so many words, nor did I, but we just became distrustful of each other.—an Illinois mother

This woman's marriage ended in divorce. We suspect the marriage of many of those who lose a baby suddenly and without apparent reason end in divorce. Blame is sometimes placed on these individuals who experience SIDS, just when they are at their weakest and most vulnerable. Some are investigated for child abuse. Public Health Nurse Janet Michel Nakushian found that often, because of the condition of the baby's body due to resuscitation methods used by distraught parents, they may be suspected of child abuse and denied needed emotional support.[1] This can be devastating for the family already weakened by the crisis of sudden infant death.

The resulting pain is not just simply guilt over the death of the baby, however. The survivors spend many of their waking hours and sleepless nights reliving every moment of their infant's short life:

I felt an overwhelming feeling of guilt, coupled with remorse. Our baby had colic from about nine days old to four weeks old. That was very difficult for me to cope with. I resented her many times and sometimes wished I'd never had her. I even had fantasies I might harm her and they surprised and upset me. She was getting to be a real pleasure to have shortly before her death at four and a half months, but I have reflected on my resentment and horrible fantasies.—a Delaware mother

For most parents there is time to outlive such negative feelings toward their children; none of us are perfect parents and there are countless things we could have done better and do try to correct. But for these parents, they must learn to live with their feelings and failings.

Too often we found many of these parents still isolated in their guilt, being unable or in some instances not allowed to verbalize their feelings:

Thirty-seven years have passed, and until four years ago I was not allowed to talk about it. Not to my husband and family or friends. I wasn't allowed to talk or cry myself out. No one wanted to know. I was blamed for letting the baby sleep on his stomach. I am seventy-two years old, and not until recently when a friend of my daughter's had a neighbor who went through the same thing was I finally able to talk and receive some comfort.

—a Missouri mother

Sudden, unexpected infant death is the major cause of death for infants between the ages of one week and one year in this country. Seven to ten thousand infants die of SIDS annually in the United States alone.[2] The deaths occur suddenly, with no warning. The term, *Sudden Infant Death Syndrome,* coined in the medical professions to describe the event, conveys a definite condition and is useful in reinforcing the idea that no guilt can be attached to the caregivers of the infant.

Still, for all the effort, the physicians find that they are not immune to guilt feelings when an infant in their care suddenly dies. "What did I miss?" is often a question they ask themselves. One young resident in a family-practice program talked to us about how he felt:

It's very emotionally draining. We want to give support and encouragement. These parents have been doing everything right, doing a super job. Then they bring the baby in and there's no heart beat. You feel terrible. You feel like you just want to leave. When the result turns out to be SIDS, you know there was nothing more that you could do, but it is emotionally draining. I cried, and went home and talked about it with my wife. My wife is pregnant and it really hit home in that regard, too.

You can return to work the next day because you know the statistics. You're playing the odds and you know that ninety-nine times out of one hundred things are going to go well. To return to work and see other mothers with small children is kind of a lift to me. Much of medicine is saddening, seeing people with a chronic disease, heart attack, something that can't be cured. In pediatric care things are usually happy. You realize that everything is not that way, and you've had excellent results in the past. You count on the success in the future.

There is an element of guilt in both the parents and the physician when something like this happens, because you think, "Oh my God, did I miss something on the exam." The autopsy kind of helps absolve everybody. At times you're seeing so many people and going so fast you wonder if you've missed something and you feel terrible when the baby dies. You can use the autopsy to help reassure them that it wasn't something they could have prevented, and to reassure yourself that there was nothing you as a physician could have done.—an Illinois physician

The same kind of what ifs come back to haunt the parents who have lost a child to SIDS. This is fairly common with most people who are grieving over some kind of loss. But there is a difference: an infant is a small bundle of potential with a future stretching out before him; an infant has not lived long and achieved but is still in the process of becoming.

When an elderly person dies, the grieving family can look back on his life and say, "Ah, but what a life he lived." With an infant there is always the possibility of what might have been. Every time a child is encountered that is the age the child would have been, the parents are left wondering, "What would my child have been like? What if he had not died?"

Notes

1. J.M. Nakushian, "Restoring Parents' Equilibrium after Sudden Infant Death," *American Journal of Nursing* 76 (1976):1600–1604.

2. J.B. Beckwith, The Sudden Infant Death Syndrome, DHEW Publication no. HSA 75–5137. (U.S. Government Printing Office, 1978).

The Research

To preserve parents' privacy and anonymity and insure contact with a large and heterogeneous group of people, we chose mailed questionnaire techniques for most of the research. Although our contact with the majority of the families who experienced the death of a child was through anonymous questionnaires rather than personal contact, we quickly began to get a sense of the tremendous crisis that had occurred in these families.

The questionnaire was thirteen pages long, beginning with four open-ended questions that allowed the participants to express in narrative form their feelings about SIDS and the crisis in their families. The remainder of the instrument consisted of questions that were adapted from the literature of family-crisis studies, death, and bereavement; from clinical impressions in the medical literature of the effects of SIDS on surviving family members; and from our own exploratory interviews with several SIDS parents. More than a dozen professionals in pediatrics, social work, child development, and family studies critiqued the questionnaire. Its validity and reliability were further enhanced by piloting with a Nebraska statewide SIDS parents' group. Over the five-year period, the instrument has undergone at least as many major revisions, tightening up and addition of questions.

In the first study in Nebraska, during January of 1976, a questionnaire was sent to every parent who could be contacted who had experienced SIDS between 1, January 1973 and 30, June 1975. Ninety-one cases of SIDS had been identified during that period by contacting the physician or coroner involved in the incident. This was done in cooperation with the Nebraska State Department of Health, Division of Maternal and Child Health, under the direction of Dr. Robert Grant. It was found that the death certificates in some of these cases showed the death to be attributable to some other cause, and the parents had not been notified that their child actually died of SIDS. Those parents who had not been notified that their child died of SIDS were not asked to participate in the study. Parents of sixty-three out of ninety-one cases were sought for the study.

Two professional staff members of the Department of Health tried to contact the parents by telephone in each of the sixty-three cases. If the parents could not be located, another telephone number with the same last name in the community was tried with hopes of locating a relative. A grand-parent was located in four cases, but in all four instances the grandparent would not allow the Department of Health to talk directly to the parents because they felt it would unnecessarily upset the parents. One grandparent stated that the couple had separated as a result of the death. Another stated that an arrest had been made after the death and the couple was still involved with the legal problems. A third grandparent stated that the hus-band had left the wife because he blamed her for the death. This grand-parent made it clear that she also blamed the mother. The fourth grand-parent indicated that her daughter, a single mother, was in the hospital at the time of the study. Because of the difficulty we had in locating parents, we began to assume a high level of disorganization in these families resulting from the death.

All fifty parents that were contacted agreed to participate in the study. However, this is a sample of only 50 percent of the families who had expe-rienced a SIDS death during that time. Of the fifty, thirty-two completed the questionnaire.

Using a similar procedure in September 1977, all families experiencing SIDS in Nebraska between 1, July 1975 and 1, January 1977 were contacted by Lorene Wood, maternal and child health counselor and nurse. Thirty-seven of seventy-four parents filled out questionnaires in this sample.

In the spring of 1979, a third study was begun. We attempted to obtain a national sample of families who had experienced SIDS. We also wanted to survey those families for whom a longer period of time had passed and attempt to find the long-term effects of SIDS.

The national study was done with the cooperation of newspapers and their family-life editors. Over 100 newspapers in all sections of the country were contacted, and 50 received follow-up calls. Of the 100 newspapers initially contacted, 20 ultimately ran news stories for us asking for volun-teers for the study. Ninety-three families responded and in most cases both the husband and the wife indicated they wanted to participate in the study. Forty-three individual questionnaires were returned completed for analysis.

The total number of parents participating in all three studies then was 112. Obtaining a large sample was not our goal, although we did wish to reach different geographic and socioeconomic stratas. From an empirical point of view, many researchers would point out that our sample was biased by the fact that only a certain type of person would be willing to complete the questionnaire. While this is true, for the purposes of our study it became less important to have great numbers as it was to allow parents to share with others their experiences. In this we feel we were successful, and it further reflects that SIDS is a catastrophe that can strike any family.

Other researchers may feel disappointed that the study was not tightly organized around a certain theoretical framework. For this we do not apol-ogize. As the research evolved it became of foremost importance to attend to the needs of those who had experienced a tragedy. When it is considered that possibly ten thousand infants die annually from SIDS, twenty thousand parents are affected; add to this siblings, grandparents, other relatives, and friends. The need for maintaining elegant structure in our minds diminished. The aim of the study changed completely as it became of prime importance to let those who had lost infants dictate the structure of this book.

With the written word, the parents conveyed in a powerful, moving way the experience of walking into a room to find their baby dead. The shock, guilt, and resulting disorganization in the family; the loneliness and grief, at times too large to comprehend, let alone process—these are the reasons for this book.

Within our culture it is common to ignore death and the dying. We prefer death to be antiseptic and removed from our everyday awareness. Death usually occurs in the hospital, on the battlefield, or on the highway. It is a rare occurrence for an individual to come suddenly upon death.[1] This is the experience we wrote about.

Medical research is looking into several different areas that might lead to an answer to what causes SIDS, but these answers are slow in coming. Our concern here focuses on the catastrophic effects such a death can have on the family. We have no easy answer as to how people should attempt to cope with the death; there is no magic cure for sorrow. But through the experiences of those who participated in this research, we hope to share and educate others about this devastating ordeal.

The babies that pass quietly from this life leave behind bewildered, confused, and often angry families:

> It has been almost a year now and we still have a hard time going into his room. It is hard to look at other babies, and I find myself looking for his face on other babies. He was my only child. I miss him terribly. Every holiday just reminds me of what I had thought about the year before. Thinking that would be the last holiday my husband and I would spend alone.

> At first I cried every day. Then, I just had an overall sadness intrude on all the times that would have been extremely pleasant before. We still want a baby. We wanted a boy and got one. Now we are afraid to try again.

> It has been one year, yet we have to face his birthday late in May and then his death date August first. Maybe then.—a Mississippi mother

A feeling of impotence and lack of control pervades the lives of these parents. If a baby can die suddenly from no apparent cause, anything can happen:

> I have really found out that nothing is permanent and it really scares me. If my two-and-a-half-year old oversleeps, I'm afraid to go in her room for fear of finding her dead.

I have felt the coldness of people who think if your baby dies you did
something, because babies don't just die. I have also felt the loneliness
from friends who are afraid of you. They avoid you; they don't call or visit
because they don't know what to say and you make them uncomfortable.
I've also come across the relatives who don't want to talk about the good
times we had with the baby, because from the start the baby becomes a part
of your life.

I feel so left out from people who know; they seem to try and handle you,
and I don't like it. It seems you get marked as the mother of a dead child
and it's hard to accept.—an Indiana mother

The format of this book is different from many research endeavors.
Our approach is to allow the participants in the research to relate their
experiences in their own words without the substance being distilled into an
overwhelming number of lifeless statistics. Theirs is a unique, subjective
crisis, which we will not attempt to objectify into yet another theory of the
process of grief.

The sharing of experience and the acknowledgment of crisis appears to
be more meaningful and useful to others than the hypotheses and the statistics. As marriage and family counselors and educators, we have led many
groups of people in the discussion of life's difficult problems. Sharing how
we feel and how we cope is probably the greatest gift we can give to another
person. This book, then, is a gift from 112 parents who have lost babies to
others who also may be forced to carry that terrible burden.

For the past five years, these parents from over eighty cities, towns, and
localities in the United States have shared with us their story and made this
research possible. For some, as little as three months had passed since the
loss of their child. For one, thirty-seven years had not erased the pain she
felt when her baby died.

Another purpose of the research is to expand knowledge of and shed
more light on death, a subject that is increasingly being pushed from our
lives. But death cannot be avoided; it will touch us all.

Robert Fulton wrote in "On the Dying of Death," that death, as it has
been traditionally defined, is dying.[2] Scientific knowledge has expanded the
definition of death to the point that exactly when death occurs is being
heavily debated. Death has come to be seen as a result of personal negli-
gence or as an accident; people are not supposed to just die any more.
Children most particularly fall into this category; with the proper immuni-
zations, nutrition, and loving care, infant mortality has decreased to the
point that the death of a baby is a shock not only to the family but the whole
community. A century ago, it was commonplace. Often, babies were not
named until months after birth, for they were not expected to live.

There cannot be life without death; it is unavoidable. In a time when
many parents enthusiastically embrace the notion of sex education and the

beginning of life, these same parents find themselves strangely mute on the subject of death. We have come full circle, the Reverend Edgar Jackson points out; a few generations ago parents could not talk about the beginnings of life but could honestly confront its end.[3]

If death is unacceptable, how is it possible to confront the grief that is left in its wake? Dr. Elisabeth Kübler-Ross's work on death and dying has been important for the dying and their families to come to grips with their own mortality. Kübler-Ross explored the needs of the terminally ill and their families. Death, she finds, is still a fearful, frightening happening; and the fear of death is a universal fear even if we think we have mastered it on many levels.[4] But death education for these families cannot begin with the pronouncement of a terminal illness. The families in this study did not have the luxury of time to prepare for death. It slapped them in the face at their most vulnerable point, with the end of a young life.

A third purpose of this research is to discourage the sanitizing of death. Funerals and the arrangements for them seem to be a necessary part of the acceptance of the loss of a child for these parents. Many expressed the need to see their child dead in the casket to take away the horrible memory of finding the child dead in their home. The rituals of death are important and the loss of a child cannot be handled with scant personal involvement. The majority of these parents found their infants dead. Without any previous experience they were thrust into a nightmare that is not abandoned with sleep.

In her own words, one mother from North Dakota reflects on the dilemma that faces us all on the subject of death: "I never thought babies die because everyone in our family lived to be old and gray and die after having a long and prosperous life. Well, I found out differently and I take no one for granted. I cherish each and every day I have with people I know and love, because in losing Matt I know no one has a written guarantee."

Notes

1. E. Jackson, *For the Living* (Des Moines: Channel Press, 1963).

2. R. Fulton, "On the Dying of Death," in *Explaining Death to Children,* ed. E.A. Grollman (Boston: Beacon Press, 1967).

3. E. Jackson, "The Theological, Psychological and Philosphical Dimensions of Death in Protestantism," in *Explaining Death to Children,* ed. E.A. Grollman (Boston: Beacon Press, 1967).

4. E. Kübler-Ross, *On Death and Dying* (New York: Macmillan Publishing Co., 1969).

3

Babies Don't Just Die, Do They? Searching for the Causes of Sudden, Unexplained Infant Death

"Babies don't just die, do they? Was my baby's death painful?" These are just two of the questions that consume parents after the sudden death of their infant. Research may be of some help in the future in answering more fully the first question, but so far the answer is that babies do just die.

Was my baby's death painful? Accoring to a study done by the Foundation for the Study of Infant Deaths, investigators found that in a large number of descriptions of how babies die from SIDS, these babies do not cry out as if in pain. Sometimes they simply become pale and die in their sleep; it appears that in whatever way they die, they first become unconscious. There is no indication that any victims of SIDS go through any period of prolonged pain or distress.[1]

In our research we received one story from a mother who told of nursing her infant. Thinking he had just gone to sleep, the mother stood up to put him to bed, only then noticing a lack of movement. The baby was dead.

Another mother related her experience:

> When I found my seven-week old son lying dead in my bed, I had a number of feelings. Since I was breastfeeding my son and had fed him in bed, I was sure I had smothered him. This fear was set aside when the coroner called to say it was SIDS. Thankfully my husband and I knew what SIDS is; many do not.
>
> I think my most potent emotion has been anger that I could not help my son, nor any of the other children that have died or will die.
>
> —a Minnesota mother

The evidence on SIDS is somewhat confusing. Professionals, lay persons, and family members are asking many questions that as yet have no answers. To dispel one myth may create another.

This chapter is an effort to review recent scientific investigations into the causes of SIDS, possibly allaying some fears. But at the onset we must caution you: we promise no answers and are skeptical of the almost weekly accounts of new developments heralded in the media. In fact, Dr. Bruce Beckwith, a SIDS researcher, has catalogued seventy-three theories of the causes of SIDS and notes that new ideas are being published almost on a weekly basis.[2]

Many people operate on the assumption that SIDS is a relatively new phenomenon; the results of a modern era of chemicals, pollutants, and new strains of virus. In discussing the syndrome, many middleaged individuals report that "in their day, babies didn't just die like that." Dodi Schultz, writing in *Science Digest,* discusses causes of death in New York City in 1825 when diagnoses were primitive. Causes of death included intemperance, worms, hives, and drinking cold water.[3] Diagnosis may not have been sophisticated enough to detect what we now call SIDS.

Historically, unexpected, unexplainable deaths of infants were routinely attributed to overlaying by the mother. Throughout history mothers have often slept with their infants, and if they woke and found the child dead they assumed they had lain on the child, smothering or crushing it. In the Bible we find probably the first reference to SIDS: "And this woman's child died in the night, because she overlaid it."[4]

F.H. Garrison, writing a "History of Pediatrics" notes a German placard, dated 1291, that recognized the "dangers" of mothers sleeping with their children and thereby suffocating the infants, and forbade mothers to take children under three years of age to bed with them.[5]

Because of the stupendous infant and childhood mortality rates from infectious diseases, malnutrition, and other currently preventable conditions, Beckwith believes SIDS was overshadowed in the past. He also feels that both parents and physicians were conditioned by the mortality rate to a more casual acceptance of unexpected death. From scanty references, Beckwith finds it is possible to presume that SIDS was occurring long before it was recognized and accepted as a diagnostic label. For many years, suffocation remained the prime candidate for the cause of sudden, unexpected death among infants. Medical examiners and coroners were among the first to explore and present evidence that the cause was not suffocation, which implies a preventable death.[6]

Babies don't just die or do they? What is SIDS? These are questions even the experts are asking. The definition of SIDS varies according to the researcher; however, it is usually defined as the sudden unexplained death of an infant where no cause is found through a postmortem examination.[7] It is generally felt that SIDS may encompass a number of conditions or diseases that have been classified as one entity. There is not as yet a set of positive findings that must be present to diagnose a death as SIDS. This means that at the present time nothing can be found in any autopsy that, by itself, would have caused the death.[8]

Dr. Maria Valdes-Dapena, in a review of literature on SIDS research through 1975 found that, as a group, infants who die of crib death show structural and functional abnormalities both through an autopsy and during their life that indicate they are defective physiologically in some way.[9] Valdes-Dapena cautions that in some cases infants do show physio-

Contents

logical functions that are different from normal babies; however, so far not one of these differences can be used to predict or diagnose the death.[10] In short, no one can yet predict or prevent SIDS.

One young mother from Georgia vented her frustration at all the theories floating around: "Friends try to help you find a reason for your baby dying and tell me that more babies die after being on the formula mine was on; or that there is a higher mortality rate of the babies born with a suction apparatus delivery. All they really do is tear off the scab and won't let me heal."

Could it have been the formula? Could it have been the delivery? Parents are haunted by these questions. Maybe they could have done something. Again, it must be stated there is no conclusive evidence to show any way in which parents could have prevented the death.

Research to determine causes and thus cures has been focused in several areas and relies mainly on clues. The Fourth National SIDS Conference was held in Minneapolis in 1980. At this conference Marie Valdes-Dapena pointed out some of the clues and explained how these clues have directed research.

Deaths from SIDS occur more often in winter and spring when respiratory illnesses are frequent. Autopsies have found inflammation in windpipes in a high number of SIDS deaths. This might explain why babies have difficulty in breathing, but does not explain why they die. The brain should send a signal for the baby to breathe harder.[11]

There is a higher incidence among blacks, poor families, and babies born to teenage mothers. These mothers may not have adequate nutritional standards or may encounter other problems that contribute to defects in the baby. The focus of this research has centered in the lower part of the brain that controls breathing. Again, a signal, which tells the child to breathe harder, may not get sent.[12]

Another clue, according to Valdes-Dapena, is that deaths are more frequent in infants with low Apgar or alertness scores at birth in infants born to mothers using drugs or who smoke and have premature babies. This is consistent with the brain-damage theory in that in these cases the brain may lack in oxygen.[13]

Most SIDS deaths occur when the baby is sleeping and usually occur between midnight and 9 a.m. The peak age for the death is between two and four months of age. The death occurs rapidly and the child turns blue and limp, apparently from lack of oxygen. The brain and the respiratory system work differently during sleep, and from two to four months babies start sleeping through the night. Again, clues are present but there is no definite link to brain dysfunction.[14]

There may be, as stated before, a number of conditions or diseases that cause or trigger SIDS. Valdes-Dapena, in her review of the literature in

1980, states that viral infections have been looked at as a link to SIDS. Viral infections are evident in autopsies of some babies, however not all, and therefore this is inconclusive. Valdes-Dapena also cites botulism as a possible contributor to a small number of cases that have been classified as SIDS.[15]

The most recent evidence has been found by Marco Chacon, a graduate student at the University of Maryland Sudden Infant Death Institute.[16] Postmortem studies showed elevated levels of a thyroid hormone tri-iodo-thyronine (T-3) in forty-four out of fifty victims. This may be a very important step in determining the cause and, ultimately, the cure of SIDS. At this point, however, it is not clear when the elevation of T-3 occurred. The elevation may have occurred after the death of the baby and be a consequence of some other problem. If this were the case, a screening device for high levels of T-3 would not help identify possible victims. However, if the elevation were present at birth or even some time in advance of the death, a screening device could help determine the high-risk babies. The T-3 level can be controlled by medication if, in fact, the high level could be identified some time in advance of the death.[17] This finding is not inconsistent with some of the other theories of researchers who believe T-3 has an influence on breathing and heart beat.[18]

A more hopeful note is that, in general, relative rates for SIDS are lower now than they were in 1969. This decrease parallels that for all infant deaths during the same period of time.[19]

Should the baby have been on a monitor? Currently, the hypothesis receiving much attention is that concerning the baby not breathing. In the medical field this is referred to as *apnea*. Apparently, all infants experience numerous short periods of not breathing. During sleep, if the apneatic episodes continue, then they could be responsible for some of the deaths attributed to SIDS. There are, however, three significant difficulties in using a monitor to prevent a SIDS death. First, the infant at risk cannot be definitely identified. There is no way to predict a SIDS-prone baby. Second, researchers point out that apnea monitors, such as those used in the home, detect only the presence or absence of abdominal breathing and will not sound an alarm in the event that the windpipe becomes obstructed.[20,21] Finally, at least one infant has been reported to have died of crib death while on an apnea monitor in a hospital intensive-care nursery.[22]

The paths of investigation into sudden, unexplained infant death are similar to other complex medical problems of the past. It is not a new phenomenon, but recognition of the problem did not occur until the 1950s. This led to research and a definition of the syndrome in the 1960s, and the current investigations. Highly qualified researchers are exploring a wide variety of hypotheses that may lead to a better understanding of sudden, unexpected, and unexplained infant death. Among professionals and the public, the level of awareness concerning SIDS is growing. This should help to prevent some of the problems parents have encountered in the past. But the information necessary to prevent sudden infant death in the future is still beyond our reach.

All too often, when a satisfactory reason is not found, the parents shoulder the responsibility for the infant's death. Seemingly innocent questions asked of the parents at the time of death can exacerbate the feelings of guilt. One North Dakota mother wrote: "I often question whether I neglected my son in some way, that I wasn't an attentive enough parent. I don't think the pain has ever subsided. You learn to cope with it better as time passes."

One of the overriding questions that parents ask is, "What could I have done to prevent this death?" Many parents embark on a desperate search for some cause on which blame can be placed. This is preferable to the parents blaming each other, but it is still a fruitless endeavor. With all the press that SIDS has gotten, it is no wonder that these parents have trouble living with the fact that their babies just died. But we still do not know why.

Notes

1. F.E. Camps, and R.G. Carpender, "Sudden and Unexpected Death in Infancy (Cot Death)." Report of the Proceedings of the Sir Samuel Bedson Symposium, Foundation for the Study of Infant Death, Ltd. (1970), pp. 124–128.

2. J.B. Beckwith, *The Sudden Infant Death Syndrome,* DHEW Publication no. HSA 75–5137 (U.S. Government Printing Office, 1978).

3. D. Schultz, "Researchers Disspelling the Mystery Surrounding SIDS Babies," *Science Digest* (1979):68–72.

4. 1 Kings 3:19, *Holy Bible, King James Version.*

5. F.H. Garrison, "History of Pediatrics," *Pediatrics* (1923):3.

6. J.B. Beckwith, *The Sudden Infant Death Syndrome,* DHEW Publication no. HSA 75–5137 (U.S. Government Printing Office, 1978).

7. J.B. Beckwith, "Discussion of Terminology and Definition of Sudden Infant Death Syndrome," in *Proceedings of the Second International Conference of Causes of Sudden Death in Infants,* ed. A.B. Bergman, J.B. Beckwith, and C.G. Ray (Seattle, University of Washington Press, 1970).

8. J.B. Beckwith, "The Sudden Infant Death Syndrome," *Current Problems in Pediatrics,* vol. 3, no. 1 (1973).

9. M. Valdes-Dapena, *Sudden Unexplained Infant Death, 1970 through 1975: An Evolution in Understanding,* DHEW Publication no. HSA 78–5255 (U.S. Government Printing Office, 1978).

10. M. Valdes-Dapena, "Sudden Infant Death Syndrome: A Review of of the Medical Literature, 1974–1979," *Pediatrics* vol. 66, no. 4 (1980): 597–613.

11. L. Cope, "Research Finding Clues to Crib Deaths," *Minneapolis Tribune,* 1980, June 4.

12. Ibid.

13. Ibid.

14. Ibid.

15. Valdes-Dapena, "Sudden Infant Death Syndrome," pp. 597–613.

16. J. Rowley, "Crib Death Discovery May Lead to Simple Test for the Disease," *Minneapolis Tribune,* 1981, November 6.

17. R. Henderson, Untitled press release. *Baltimore Sun* (Field News Service), 1981, November 6.

18. Cope, "Research Finding Clues."

19. Valdes-Dapena, *Sudden Unexplained Infant Death.*

20. C. Guilleminault, R. Peraita, M. Souguet, et al., "Apnea During Sleep in Infants: Possible Relationship with Sudden Infant Death Syndrome," *Science* 190 (1975):677.

21. E.G. Hasselmeyer, *Research Perspectives in the Sudden Infant Death Syndrome,* DHEW Publication no. NIH 76–1976 (U.S. Government Printing Office, 1976).

22. N. Lewak, "Sudden Infant Death Syndrome in a Hospitalized Infant on an Apnea Monitor," *Pediatrics,* 56 (1975):296.

4

"I'll Lend You for a Little While a Child of Mine." God, Guilt, and Punishment

The process that parents go through, when faced with the sudden, unexpected death of their infant, is an attempt to regain some equilibrium. The blaming and the guilt are difficult to avoid. Even if the parents, on an intellectual level, convince themselves of their lack of culpability, feelings of guilt on the emotional level still remain. When told over and over that they are not to blame and there was nothing they could have done, the individual parents still often seek answers, and the vacuum created by the lack of conclusive research can lead to tremendous guilt.

Science notwithstanding, within the social organization of our culture, the Judeo-Christian ethic is often interpreted to propound the idea that guilt decrees punishment. This tenet can be self-fulfilling. If you are punished, you must be guilty of something; you are guilty and, therefore, are being punished. One Georgian woman expressed these kinds of thoughts: "I often felt like it was something I did wrong. I guess the guilt feelings were the worst of all. It hurts when I see any of Matthew's clothes, toys, and so forth, and it still shakes me up when I hear of another crib death. I just get sick all over. Often I felt like I was being punished, but then God doesn't work that way."

Guilt and anger become confused, and the what ifs and if onlys crowd the mind.

My babysitter found our eight-week-old boy dead during an afternoon nap, and I received a call at work. At first I was hysterical, then through the funeral I was numb and for about a week after I was very sad. I felt so lonely for my Josh. I longed to hold him, and felt guilty for having said, "Oh, I hope you sleep through the night because I'm really tired."

I felt bitter toward someone, but I never did figure out who (God was in the back of my mind). Then I thought that Josh might have thought he was a great burden to us and decided to leave us. After all there is no reason for SIDS, so your mind thinks of everything.

About a week after Josh died I visited our babysitter who had found Josh, and she told me she just found out she was pregnant. For an instant I hated

her, because I felt that, "My baby died here with you and now you tell me that you will have a baby in eight months." I have trouble becoming pregnant and I am in a panic thinking I will never be able to have another baby.
—a Missouri mother

Time is usually seen as a cure-all by well-meaning friends, relatives, and professionals. But who is to judge how much time is necessary? In our study of SIDS parents, we found it took parents, on the average, thirty-six months to regain the level of personal happiness they felt they had held before the death.

In the final analysis though, each individual must determine for himself or herself how long it will take to recover:

Immediately after the death was a feeling of depression, loss of goals, and overall confusion. It still does not seem like our baby has been gone for over a year. At times I wonder if we did everything possible or whether we did something wrong; but then I remember how happy our little one was, and the good times we had and I remember her smile and laugh.

I frequent the gravesite to gaze upon the grave, look to the sky for hope, faith, and strength and to think and to maybe give myself peace of mind. In my heart I know we were not at fault, but little things remind me of her and I wonder—a Kansas mother

The *if onlys* can lead to guilt and a very real depression, the return from which can be slow and painful. At least half of the parents in the studies often or nearly always suffered the following physical and/or psychological difficulties during the crisis: trouble sleeping, nervousness and feeling fidgety and tense, loss of appetite, and difficulty getting up in the morning.

I think the worst thing is guilt, I still think that I should have stayed up with her that night, and then she'd be alive today. She had a stuffy nose, and I felt that if I had only taken her to the doctor she would have been alive. I have even gotten up in the night to check the other kids. I know that crib death can't happen to them because they're too old, but I had to get up and check them anyway.

I thought for awhile I was going to crack up. I am not a nervous person by nature but I was shaky and moody for quite awhile; I still am a little. The first few weeks after Sara died, I didn't want to get up in the morning, I guess I didn't want to face reality. Sometimes I'd think I was just having a horrible dream, and when I'd wake up, everything would be okay.

Sometimes I've thought that I'd be able to change things somehow, like if I could find out what causes crib death, I could have Sara back again. But there is always this voice in my mind telling me that it really happened, I can't change it, and I have to accept what has happened.
—an Indiana mother

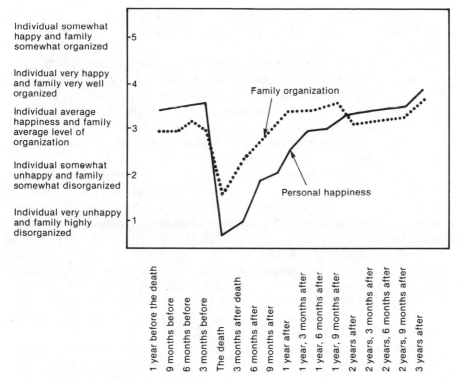

Note: Number = 112.

Figure 4-1. Mean Levels of Personal Happiness and Family Organization in Relation to the Death

Small things trigger memories, and there is no escape from the thoughts:

> This is the most painful time I have ever had to accept. It's hard to be a mother one day and not the next. The first months my arms actually ached to hold her again. I kept thinking I could hear her in bed playing, but it was just the furnace kicking on. I still miss her and find myself reliving in my mind those seven months before she died. I have just given birth to a healthy boy, but I still have fears of finding him the way I did Tammy.—
> —a Colorado mother

Sleep does not provide an escape either, as one woman from Massachusetts wrote: "I have been more nervous than before. A lot of times I can't sleep, I hear my baby crying. I also dream of going to her grave and she would be alive, sitting there playing with her sister. I wonder why my baby had to die. I have gone through a lot of hell since she died. I still feel if only I could have done something to have prevented her from dying I would have.''

The death can cause the crystallization of philosophies, which previously were formless and unspoken. An Ohio mother wrote: "In the last few years I have done a lot of soulsearching. It seems I was always looking for who I was or what my capabilities were. The death of my son left me with feelings as to what kind of mother I wanted to be. Before his death, it seems that I just was a mother with no thought behind it. Now I give a thoughtful consideration to the quality of my motherhood."

A second woman from Pennsylvania wrote: "I have gone through a period of anger and bitterness, but this has turned into a greater appreciation or an awareness of what is around me. Also, a greater understanding of other people and their lives. My values have changed from materialistic to more abstract."

God is usually not seen as the deliverer of punishment and was infrequently blamed. One Maine man stated his feelings in this way: "One thing that never occurred to me was to lash out at God for my loss. Neither did my wife. But I think others may select God as a convenient scapegoat to cover their own fears and doubts. Anyone who is undergoing this kind of crushing guilt needs the strongest faith possible."

Faith and a strong belief in God is a comfort to many, as a mother from Montana eloquently wrote: "I feel that it is God's will and my faith in God has gotten me through this. I have a saint in heaven to guide my son and me in our daily lives. My faith in God has been doubled since Kate's death, more than I would ever believed. Who else does one have to believe in if not God?"

The attitudes and opinions of others were at times detrimental to the families who had lost a child. "Things were said at the time of the death that make it harder for me. Comments about Bret not being baptized really bothered me. Even though I am not religious, I know that God lived in Bret and He hadn't deserted Bret because we neglected to baptize him," expressed one Pennsylvania mother.

Often, well-thought-out plans can be turned inside out by the sudden, unexplained death of a child:

This pregnancy was not planned, and at first it was very upsetting due to the fact that my husband was in school and would be for two years after the birth of the baby; however, after several days we both had our heads on straight and were happy about it. At the time of birth we considered our family complete with a boy and a girl.

I was very insistent about not wanting any more children; in fact it got to be an obsession with me and my husband, and I decided to take measures to be sure we did not have any more. Approximately seven weeks after the birth of our son, I got it in my head that I was pregnant again and was very upset and hard to live with. My doctor tried to convince me that I wasn't, but I couldn't be convinced so he did a menstrual extraction. After this is when we decided to take measures so as not to have any more children. My husband had a vasectomy. Approximately two weeks after the doctor told him the vasectomy was a success, our baby died.

The way I had acted after his birth in not wanting any more children really had an impact on me mentally after he died. I felt I was being punished for being so insistent and definite on what I wanted. After he died, I immediately realized that I did not know for sure that I didn't want another baby, so my husband made arrangements with a doctor to have his vasectomy reversed.

I didn't get pregnant. As time went on the desire to have another baby became less and less, and after about a year I decided that things happen for the best. My husband still wanted another baby, but I was to the point it didn't really matter. We talked about adoption, but never pursued it. In time I had to have a hysterectomy, so that settled the question of my trying to get pregnant.

I look back over all that we went through and it seems like a dream. "Things like that always happen to someone else" was what I kept thinking. There were good days and bad days as with anything else. It has been three-and-a-half years since his death and it is hard for me to remember the exact feelings each day. All I can say is that it was bad, there is no easy way out for anyone who is faced with this kind of crisis, only time can heal.

I have learned to accept the fact that my baby is gone, but I don't think I will ever really get over it or understand why it happened. I never really thought about death very much prior to this, neither looking forward to it or dreading it; but now when I think about death I get a very special kind of comfort in coping with our loss.

It has been a most heartbreaking experience, but one that time and faith have helped to heal. A friend gave me a poem that I read daily and it proved to be very comforting and helpful to me, a portion of which I'll quote:

> "I'll lend you for a little while a child of mine,"
>   God said,
> "For you to love while he lives, and mourn for when
>   he's dead;
> It may be six or seven years, or twenty-two or
>   three,
> But will you 'til I call for him, take care of him
>   for me. . ."

a Pennsylvania mother

When Is It My Turn to Cry?
The Father Grieving

Do men react differently than women to the death of a child? Currently, the popular notion of the inexpressive male would have us believe that men suffer a deficit in being unable to verbalize their feelings.

Starting in the preschool years, males often are told to be strong, to hold back tears, to tough it out in silence. Role models for the growing boy are often macho types: athletes and television action heroes. It would be little wonder, then, if men did react with quiet sobriety, playing a Gary Cooperesque, stoic part. And in fact, in our studies fewer men did participate in filling out the questionnaires (about 40 percent of the total), and those who did wrote less than the women. Yet it is quite difficult to quantify the depth of their feelings, and impossible to deny that these feelings exist. One man from Ohio typified the responses we received from men when he wrote, "I have almost forgotten what has happened. I miss him very much and it feels like a dream. That's about all I want to say, I'm not much on writing."

Some men wrote one or two words, usually about guilt and fear, and then added that they were not very open with emotions or feelings. We found one man that wanted to be open but because of pressures he felt he could not. This is how he expressed himself:

> All of us have heard of how one event or another will turn a person's life around or how a tragedy will disrupt the lives of many people. With little or no warning, the lives of several people can be changed, overturned, or redirected because of one fateful event. This is exactly what happened to my wife, family, friends, and me on a Sunday three months ago. In a matter of seconds our cheerful, gay vacation supper turned into a tearful struggle to bring life back into our young daughter's body.

> Immediately following the discovery of Jennifer's lifeless body, the tears that flowed were of horror, fear of the truth, and disbelief. My tears as I tried to revive our baby were a mixture caused by total confusion between a fear of disbelief and a fear of not wanting to know what was evident before my eyes, lying in my arms. As we accompanied Jenny to the hospital and held her for the last time, the tears and statements were directed to her but were really spoken selfishly for each of us. Being religious enough to believe God had Jenny with Him and she would have a greater peace with Him than we could ever provide, each of us was crying for our loss, the loss of a beautiful baby girl.

Throughout the next few days we were protected by our families from intrusions and problems that the arrival of many friends and acquaintances can bring. During this time, however, we insisted on making the decisions for Jennifer's funeral and appropriate arrangements because she was ours. So together Chris and I decided what dress Jenny was to be buried in, what type of casket to purchase, where we should plan and purchase our family plots, and similar decisions that seemed to go on and on. These were decisions I had never thought about before which were difficult to decide on then and hard to think about now.

Finally Jenny was buried with the blessings of family, friends, and parents. Everyone had to regroup in their own special way so that they might continue to live productive lives. For days after Jenny's death we were visited by people who wished us well and extended appropriate sympathy. Slowly the tears seemed to disappear as our natural defense mechanisms came forward to push the despair down deeper so as to allow for self-preservation.

Our return home to Minot was tearful and somewhat frightening as the loneliness was reinforced and reality's cruelty became terribly apparent. Friends and colleagues trying to be kind or simply protect themselves would ignore the subject of Jennifer and the entire situation concerning her death. This natural tendency for everyone to ignore the subject for fear of bring up tender memories created hostility in both Chris and me. We loved Jennifer while she was with us and we continue to love her though she is no longer with us; ignoring her was insulting something very important in our lives. I was hurt then and to some degree criticize this action now; but, more than three months ago if I were confronting a friend who had lost a baby, fear of saying something wrong would probably have kept me from talking of the subject also.

Those people who would comment about Jenny's death would say how sorry they were and then ask how my wife was. This concern for Chris was appreciated, for she was terribly shaken by Jennifer's death. Along with concern for Chris' well-being came words of wisdom or advice as to my conduct or how to handle my wife in this situation. People advised me to handle Chris with great care for this was a loss like nothing she would ever have encountered before. "Show her great patience, more than ever before, be kind to her, and be extremely understanding."

The needs of my wife were well known to me during this ordeal and I felt I was prepared to follow through with my obligation to stand by her and help. Suddenly, however, just two weeks after Jennifer's death, I realized that for some reason I was expected to be the strength of our relationship. I was supposed to provide great amounts of support for my mourning wife and show her greater patience and love then ever before. Everywhere I turned I received this same advice. Only two people mentioned concern for me during this period. This feeling began to bother me after a while for it seemed that I was either supposed to not show any emotion about the death of our daughter or I was simply to be able to go through this ordeal without having it affect me, thereby not needing the period of mourning that was afforded my wife.

Strong feelings surfaced: "Doesn't anyone care about me? Jennifer was part of me, too, you know. When is it my turn to cry?" I became sensitive.

I sensed people were telling me it was all right for me to have cried immediately following Jennifer's death, but now my mourning must stop and I
should be able to repel those strong emotions and be a man for my wife,
family, and society. My.wife was allowed a period to not be herself, but I
was expected to go back to work upon our return and function as though
nothing had happened. My tender defense emotions quickly turned into a
feeling of hostility toward society in general as it somehow told me I
couldn't really be myself, I couldn't cry anymore, I must be strong, I must
be a man.

In dealing with Jennifer's death I could and can cry with my wife in the
security of our home and feel only a slight bit of embarrassment, since crying is unusual in my family and opposes my basic nature. My basic manly
nature is not to be one to show much emotion, but I still can cry and release
those strong emotions within the confines of my home. Nowhere else have I
encountered such freedom.

Following Jennifer's death, I saw my father cry for the first time in my life.
Her death shook this pillar of strength to an emotional state I don't believe
he ever knew before. My father felt badly about this emotional state and
the afternoon before Jennifer's funeral as we stood in our front yard, he
apologized for not being stronger. He was truthful when he said, as he
sobbed, how he expected and wanted himself to be the strength and resolv-
ing force to guide us through this tragedy, but he just couldn't. He had
never experienced such a helpless feeling and it was hard for him to accept
that feeling.

I recall telling my father that I could expect no more out of any father than
for him to be himself. Jennifer had touched everyone who had known her
with the special love that was unique to her and my father was expressing
his loss of that love with his tears. This conversation and display of emotion was a unique experience for both of us and I doubt if we will ever find
a situation where we will freely discuss our true emotions with each other
again. For even now I know I have allowed my defenses to build up and
protect me and not allow me to talk totally freely, even with this very special man.

When is it my turn to cry? I'm not sure society or my upbringing will allow
me a time to really cry, unafraid of the reaction and repercussion that
might follow. I must be strong, I must support my wife because I am a
man. I must be the cornerstone of our family because society says so, my
family says so, and until I can reverse my learned nature, I say so.

—a Nebraska father

Allowing men to feel and express their grief would be, according to
some family-life theorists and not a few feminists, very healthy. This is all
well and good; but then men would be placed in a double bind, no-win
situation. The same people who consider a man calloused and unfeeling if
he does not fall apart over the death of a child may turn their back with discomfort when a man does fall apart. Our rhetoric has not caught up with
acceptable practice, and men are trapped in between.

Some men in the study were angry. We asked the question, "What things have people done during this time that have made it harder for you?" One man from New York answered, "The coroner asking for an inquest at my expense, just so there wouldn't be hard feelings between my wife and myself. And second and biggest, people like you sending bullshit like this questionnaire to remind us of the loss of our son. Don't do it again!

For some men the death of a child was a catalyst for change in their lives. "The death made me assess where I was and what I wanted to do. I left the Air Force where I had a good career started so I could pursue personal goals. Our daughter's death allowed me a chance to feel and express emotions for the first time in my life," expressed an Illinois father.

Many men expressed a helpless feeling at being unable to console their wives and were grateful to those who were there to help. Others found it more difficult to accept help, as one father from Colorado put it: "The hardest thing was to see the feelings of others when they came to offer assistance, and so forth. I could see they felt pity and helplessness, and it was difficult for me to keep my composure under this stress."

Men feel as deeply as women, but the vehicle for expression is often missing. Just to tell a man, "It's all right, go ahead and cry," is hardly enough. As one Montana man related to us, "People told me to cry and let it all out, but I really don't know how. Perhaps it will come in time. Meanwhile, I will have to deal with it the best way that I know."

Dreams die with the death of a child. One Ohio father discovered on the death of his child that, "I guess you'd call it a slight depression. I sort of had dreams of a son taking over my farm some day."

Another man expressed similar feelings: "I felt anger, loss of patience, intermittent grief, difficulty in praying. Prior to his death, a very strong religious base. The fact that all a person's plans, dreams, goals, and so forth can be ended so suddenly without the person involved being able to do a thing about it."

Daily reminders are present that prevent an individual from just putting out of mind the tragedy that has occurred:

> We were planning and taking for granted so much. Even yet, about a year later, things come up which we secretly promised to give or live with her, which is of course impossible now.

> We live in a rural community and know a lot of people. We see on the street my wife's roommate from the hospital with her youngster, growing, starting to talk and walk. Seeing or hearing a little baby or the one that was born at the same time is very hard to take. We will probably always watch this one grow up, especially on important days in his life, like birthdays and graduation, because that is how old ours would have been.
>
> —a Montana father

Relatives, in their zeal to protect the father from painful memories, many times do more harm than good, as a father from Pennsylvania told us: "When you try to talk to relatives about Debbie they will change to something else, like she never was a part of our life. In seventeen months not one relative, after the first month, has said, 'Well how are you getting along now?'"

The idea that men are not sensitive is refuted by the testimony of one distraught father from New Jersey: "The hardest thing is for me to hear our daughter's grandmothers making over and bragging about their other grandchildren. I guess I am selfish, but maybe we can have some kids for the grandmothers, someday, too."

Another Pennsylvania man faced a different problem: "The hardest is trying to explain what SIDS is because people always say, 'Yes, I know about SIDS, but what did she die of?'"

The feeling of impotence the death of a very young child engenders in our culture at large can have devastating effects on the parents of these children. Everybody wants an answer they can live with; and the notion that a child just dies without apparent reason is unacceptable to many. One father from Illinois stated, "Some people have made comments that would indicate they felt we had been doing something wrong to cause the child's death."

Another father from New Jersey, after the death of his child had been attributed to SIDS encountered this problem. "The funeral director tried to make us feel guilty. He told us the child had died of pneumonia, and made strong suggestions that lack of care was the problem. I'm not sure why he behaved so poorly, possibly because we had a very low-key burial."

One man explained his feelings this way:

Everyone tries to be helpful and say it's okay, everything will be all right. But it's not, and nobody can make everything all right but yourself and time.

It seems that some of my friends were afraid to talk about their kids in front of me. They would start and then stop in midsentence. Also they would visit us at our house and not bring their babies, thinking they were doing us a favor.

People should not try to be street-corner doctors and talk about SIDS when they don't understand it, because I don't understand it and I have read everything I could find on it.—a Delaware father

The passage of time for some men adds a certain perspective to such a loss, as a California father expressed: "It has been five years now and it is a bittersweet memory. For the first few months it was a shocking, almost unbearable experience. The first year there was always a sense of loss and emptiness. Now there are the good memories mixed with the feelings of a sort of life unfulfilled. We all consider him to still be a part of our family.''

The original question still remains unanswered. Do men react differently than women to the loss of a child? Men stated feelings of anger more often than women. Women react with sorrow and depression more often than men. Also, men expressed a stronger desire to keep their mourning a private matter within the family. They also stated more feelings of fear and a loss of control.

As figure 4–1 shows, it took parents an average of about thirty-six months to regain the former level of happiness they had before the baby died. In analyzing men's responses compared to women's, the reader can see in figure 5–1 that both sexes take about the same time to recover—a long time.

Family organization is defined as how well people function together in the family unit. Individuals were asked to chart their family's level of organization at various time intervals after the death of their baby. Figure 5–2

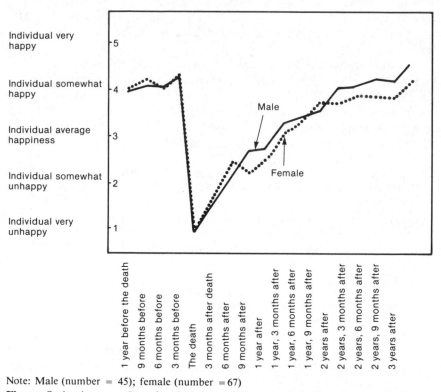

Note: Male (number = 45); female (number = 67)

Figure 5–1. Average Levels of Personal Happiness in Relation to the Death

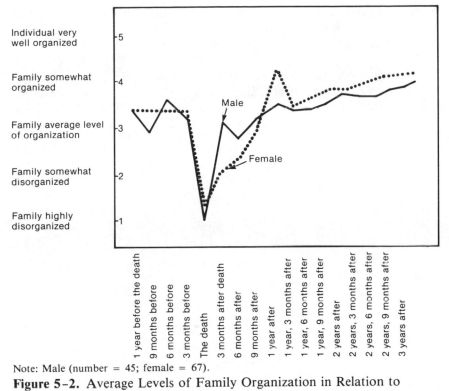

Individual very
well organized

Family somewhat
organized

Family average level
of organization

Family somewhat
disorganized

Family highly
disorganized

Note: Male (number = 45; female = 67).

Figure 5-2. Average Levels of Family Organization in Relation to
the Death

shows that both men and women felt the family had returned to its former level of organization an average of one year after the death.

Because men and women often have different styles of communication and coping with grief, marital discord is quite possible after the death of a baby. Men, taught to be strong and silent, often baffle and anger women, who learned to be open and emotional. This can lead to tremendous conflict and, on occasion, divorce.

Some professionals working with families who have experienced SIDS guess the divorce rate to be 40 to 70 percent. As researchers we believe it is impossible to know for sure; simply because no one has been able to randomly sample SIDS families. Even with a reasonably complete list of SIDS families in Nebraska, we were only able to find about 50 percent of these people. None were divorced. But others had moved away and could not be contacted. How many of them divorced? There is no way to find out for sure.

Our guess is that many marriages do end after the death of a baby.

Marriage is a fragile relationship, threatened on many fronts. But the death does not have to kill the marriage. As we demonstrate later in this book, many families are stronger—not weaker—after they recover from the death.

We urge people to seek professional help if they feel the family's stability is threatened after the death. Sometimes counseling can make a tremendous difference. A local SIDS group is a good place to start looking for counselors. The SIDS parents will know who they think can help.

6

What Should I Say to a Grieving Person?

What can you say to a bereaved parent? What can you do to help? The answers to these questions are not easy to come by. What might be helpful for one person might provoke anger from another. The reaction is often dependent on the individual personality, on the setting, and on the time and place.

For example, one woman pointed out:

> Nobody can know exactly what to say to a grieving parent. Things that at the time may seem right can be very wrong. A simply "I'm sorry" can mean so much. A hug or tear also helps the parent to realize that the grief is not totally his or hers.

> I didn't like my mother-in-law's attitude or martyrdom. She acted as though she was the only one who cared. My parents couldn't understand her attitude, and they were truly grieving also. When we found that we are expecting again, my mother-in-law cried. She wanted to know how we could think of ever replacing Timmy. She can't understand that Timmy can never be replaced.—an Arizona mother

Individuals, in an effort to ease the pain these parents suffer can make the mistake of treating the infant as a renewable resource.

> People have told me that I was lucky that I didn't have her any longer than I did. Or they say, "Just be glad it wasn't one of your older children," as if it makes some difference how long you have your child, to decide how much it should hurt to lose it. Also some people told my husband and me about every person they knew who had ever lost a child or more than one child. All this on the day of the funeral. Right then I didn't care about anyone else and anything else. I knew these people probably meant well, but I can still hear some of the things they said.

> I had a tubal ligation done after Sara was born; she was our fourth child. People told me that it was God's way of punishing me for having the surgery done.—a Connecticut mother

Ignorance, fear, and thoughtfulness can account for some of the things that are said that hurt these parents, but at times there seems to be no discernible reason for what people do say:

In the hospital a woman came up to my family. She looked at me and asked, "What happened, did he suffocate in his pillow?"

When I was pregnant with our next child a man came up to my husband and said, "Well, maybe she will do better next time."

After three more children, we finally found the time to plan a trip alone and the children's grandmother was going to watch them, but my sisters-in-law objected because the other baby had died. Our youngest child was a year old at the time.—a Nevada mother

It is evident from the responses of 112 parents that a person's presence is important to them. What the person says does not have to be particularly profound, for who knows, really, what to say?

Some people tend to keep you feeling upset because they avoid you, because they don't know what to say or do. Some people act like they don't believe that SIDS exists. They want you to give another reason why she died so young. People also have said things like, "I guess it was better she died so young because you would have been more attached to her later in life." Others have said, it was God's way of punishing us for our wrong way of life.—a Nebraska mother

Keeping ideas on the causes of SIDS to ourselves is particularly important. Only those who have actually experienced a SIDS death in their families should offer to share their stories; just having known someone that it happened to is not enough. If hundreds of researchers and millions of dollars have not produced answers to why the babies died, it is foolish of us to further perplex the grieving parents with our silly theories and folktales.

Each family is unique and this affects the way in which they handle a crisis. Some families express a desire to be left alone. "After the funeral we needed time to be alone as a family and we had relatives linger on. They were from out of state and it made it difficult for us to grieve alone as a family," said a New Jersey mother.

Other families expressed a need to be surrounded constantly by relatives and friends:

Let the person suffering the death talk. I know myself, I need to talk. I don't want other people to forget Sara. I need to know that other people remember her, too. I have to tell people how I feel, I need to know that they really want to listen and not to feel that I'm going crazy because I need to tell people about it.

Some people get upset when I mention the baby's name. They tell me to forget about it. I will never forget.—a Pennsylvania mother

It is simply not true that if we do not talk about something it will go away:

People should try to talk from time to time about the child with the grieving couple—the good memories of his life. This helps the couple accept the
child's life as well as death. It seemed that many of our friends and relatives
go to great lengths in a roundabout way not to say our child's name or refer
to his death. Also their uneasiness to say the word died or funeral only adds
to the discomfort of the situation.—a Pennsylvania mother

Another woman from Nebraska expressed similar feelings: "The most
important thing that people can do is to talk to me. I understand that it's
uncomfortable for them to hear me talk about a child that was so young and
that nobody knew. But he lived and we loved him and will never forget. It
hurts not to talk about him."

These parents are often understanding of our discomfort and sensitivity
to death, and it would seem that as concerned friends and relatives we
should try to do something even if it may turn out wrong. We must take the
risk and hope that we can be of some help. As a mother from Nevada said:
"The worst thing to do is to be afraid to say anything for fear it may be the
wrong thing. We know how awkward people feel at the time, trying to comfort us. But just the fact that someone cares enough to call, write, or visit
makes us feel better. Even if they didn't say just the right words, it helped
just because they cared."

Small things affect individuals in different ways. "I felt that if one
more person said they were sorry I would scream. I knew they are sorry, but
it doesn't bring our baby back," noted an Illinois mother.

It is very hard for these parents to see and hear other babies after losing
their own. One woman explained.

People that had new babies would avoid me or have someone keep their
babies while they came to see me. Don't avoid me! It hurts at first to see a
woman with her baby because I can't understand why she can have her
babies and I can't have mine. The thought that helped me most was that
God had His reason for taking Brian. And I have the peace of mind to
know that he didn't suffer, because I was holding him in my arms and he
just went to sleep. He didn't cry or struggle, he just went peacefully to
sleep.—a Delaware mother

The very nature of the tragedy leaves the parents and family raw and
bleeding. They are generally not well informed about SIDS, and in the days
that follow the numbness and loss of reality is not a good time for a crash
course on the causes of SIDS. As one Iowa father put it, "For me death
always has a cause-and-effect relationship. When people are old and have a
heart attack, they're supposed to die. Four-month old babies are not supposed to die." His bewilderment and grief left him confused and angry and
not at all receptive toward others who were also seeking an answer.

Many families are given a certain amount of time in which to mourn.

Although the length of time is never specific, future plans for the family are based on their return to "normal." Comments such as, "Don't feel like you have to come back to work until things are back to normal," can leave the family wondering just exactly what is normal, and how long it takes to get there. A family that suffers a death will never return to the same place they were before the death; not entirely, anyway, for a crisis forces change on some level. The situation may become better or even worse, but never the same.

John Wanzenreid has worked intensively with SIDS parents and concluded in his article on "What to Say and What Not to Say to the Sudden Infant Death Syndrome Parent" that:

> The public can take some active steps to help. As a friend, take time to read the literature on Sudden Infant Death. You can then explain to friends and relatives of the grieving parents that the baby died of SIDS. Let everyone understand that current medical science recognizes nothing can prevent the death. There is no recognized cause. No amount of supervision can prevent a baby's death. Knowledge about sudden infant death—that it's the single biggest killer of children, ages birth to one year, can do a great deal toward understanding and acceptance of death from this syndrome.[1]

For these parents to get to the place where they can rejoice at the time they did have with their baby is a slow, painful process. These parents cannot necessarily speed up the process of healing by having or not having another baby. It is not accomplished by well-meaning friends or relatives removing all signs of the baby from the grief-stricken home, unless it is at the request of the parents. Friends, who allow the parents to express doubts, to cry, to vent all of the bottled-up emotions of hostility and anger without rejecting them or denying their pain, help the parents put their confused worlds back into order.

One woman illustrated the confusion of family and friends as to what they should say and do:

> Everyone from doctors, friends, relatives and ministers all were so helpful. We have many beautiful and loving people in our lives and they did and have done everything possible for us. The main thing is no matter when or where I needed someone to talk to there was always someone there.
>
> The only thing that might have bothered me is sometime I would need to be alone to think things through and then a houseful of company would come that I could have done without for the time being; but they had no way of knowing I was feeling that way at the time.—a Delaware mother

Most people want to be helpful and not add to the pain the parents are already experiencing. But SIDS parents have to learn to accept some uncomfortable situations, such as a casual acquaintance asking how the baby is a month after she died. And even though done through sheer ignorance, pain is often felt when SIDS parents are asked how many children they have. To not count the dead child causes feelings of guilt; but how many times can these parents explain what happened? They are sensitive to the fact that other people think they are morbid for remembering a child, and yet to find peace of mind they cannot reject their baby's existence. They are, thus, in a double bind: Should they make others feel uncomfortable about a topic most of us would rather avoid? Or, should they try to honestly express their feelings and perhaps be judged as not mourning properly?

What works in one situation might not work in another. One mother felt great comfort to think that her baby was an angel; but another mother rejected this notion angrily, saying. "I didn't want an angel, I wanted a baby." Statements that, "At least the baby didn't suffer," can sometimes provoke a living nightmare of thoughts: "Did he cry out and I didn't hear him? Did he struggle and suffer alone? How will I ever know? Many of these parents in the loneliness of sleepless nights often remember and micro-scopically examine what relatives, friends, and professionals say to them.

In conclusion, while there is no simple formula for "what to say or do for a grieving parent," there are some things that we communicate verbally or nonverbally that can help restore their peace of mind. It's important to say, "I care," "I will be here if you need me," "Let me do those dishes" (or make beds or whatever you can see needs to be done). The family might really need you weeks later, after the company is gone and the last covered dish has been returned. A call, "Come to dinner," or "Let's go to a movie," can help move the family into interaction with others they have been avoiding because they just do not know how to start again.

We must be prepared for outrage, anger, guilt, as well as other responses as we try to comfort a bereaved parent. Most of the parents felt they were able to discern the difference between those who were honest and caring and the more self-righteous, unusually self-serving individuals. If we genuinely care, it will come through no matter how we fumble along. It is okay to cry because these parents feel they are sharing their grief and not that they are making us feel bad. It is perfectly natural to feel bad when a baby dies, so leave the stiff upper lip at home. Follow the cues given by the parents and do not insist on entertaining them with stories of other trag-edies, unless we also have directly experienced the death of a child. It is essential to explore our own feelings about death and come to terms with what we are comfortable with. Our genuineness will come through.

The major burden for recovery, however, falls on the mothers and fathers who have lost children. As badly as we may want to help them, they alone must learn to live with the guilt, anger, and sadness of the sudden, unexpected death of a child.

Note

1. J. Wanzenreid, "What to Say and What Not to Say to the Sudden Infant Death Syndrome Parent." Manuscript. Department of Communication, University of Nebraska at Omaha, Omaha, Nebraska, 1980.

**Friends, Relatives,
and Professionals**

I was accused of killing the baby. I was told that babies don't just die like that. Some people told me I had too many children anyway.
—a Nevada Mother

I wasn't a good mother; if I would have taken better care of my baby she would have lived. I am being punished by God for something I have done.
—a Connecticut mother

While death touches all of us eventually, we remain uncomfortable with the subject. This discomfort clearly surfaces when a death occurs in our family, in a friend's family, or if we come in contact with death as a professional.

Our attitudes, biases, and knee-jerk reactions to the families involved with the sudden, unexplainable death of an infant—all these set the stage for how the family will understand and learn to cope with such a tragedy.

Ignorance of SIDS is much of the problem with individual responses to these families, as one woman, whose three-month-old baby died, pointed out:

> People insisted that the child would have been retarded had he lived, that maybe it was best that he died. People who knew almost nothing about SIDS have read or heard that a certain position during sleep would have prevented the death. Knowing what they do, they believe that they will never have to worry about a "crib death."

> Agencies haven't been much help. I wrote letters and never received any replies. It took five months to get the SIDS charms I ordered. The people in my community that are SIDS parents talk a lot, but when it comes to action, trying to get some standard procedure when a crib death occurs— they are too busy.—a West Virginia mother

This, of course, is not always the case, and many communities have instituted programs and procedures to be followed when the death of an infant occurs. For example, Nebraska has established a protocol for SIDS counselors. Written by the Nebraska SIDS Project it says:

After a suspected SIDS death, a counselor will be notified by the county attorney, a representative from his office, or the SIDS Project office. Once notified, the counselor will follow the SIDS protocol.

The counselor will phone the physician to explain his or her role in supporting the family, learn what the family has been told concerning the death, and ask about other pertinent family history.

The counselor will then contact the family by phone or make a visit to the home to leave a pamphlet and set up an appointment for another visit.

The purpose of the first visit is to provide the family with verbal and written facts about the disease, Sudden Infant Death Syndrome; begin to allay their guilt in the death of their child; and provide support during this tragic crisis, if possible. This visit is made within forty-eight hours of the death. It may be a short visit due to the emotional state of the family. The counselor should be an empathic listener and alert to the family's needs. The family's support system should be identified. The nurse may also be a liaison for the family with the physician, mortician, minister, and other friends and family members. The counselor must remain alert to abnormal or extreme reactions and should not hesitate to contact the mental-health professionals for case consultation or referral when indicated. The counselor should leave his or her name and phone number with the family as well as a few copies of the facts pamphlets. Arrangements should be made for the next contact.

One to two weeks after the death a phone call to the family will be helpful in assessing the family's current situation and arrangements can be made for the next home visit. At this point, the counselor should also verify that the family has been made aware of the preliminary autopsy results. This is to be noted on the report and referral form.

The second home visit should be made within a month of the death. This visit will be for the purpose of reinforcing the information the family received during the first visit and assessing their progress in working through the grief process. They were probably in a state of shock and disbelief when the initial visit was made and unable to absorb all of the information given them.

The family may now be functioning in the longing and preoccupation stage. They may have fears of "going crazy" because they "hear" the infant cry, begin to fix his meals or their arms simply ache to hold their baby. As the grief process is explained, their fears may be relieved. Other physical and emotional symptoms of grief may be identified. The counselor should also be aware of the effect the death has had on the marital relationship and the surviving siblings.

A follow-up home visit may be made at three or six months at the discretion of the counselor. The ongoing process of grief may be assessed to determine how well the family is functioning at this time. The family may also be interested in subsequent children. Information regarding SIDS and heredity, SIDS and apnea monitoring, or discussion of the fears and anxieties parents experience with a subsequent pregnancy and infant may be topics to include . . .

Because the grief reaction may intensify on the anniversary or birthdate of the baby, a phone call may be beneficial for the family. The family may also be encouraged to phone the counselor at the time of a subsequent pregnancy for support and/or information. . . .[1]

Parent-support groups are also seen as very helpful by many families. One woman from Nebraska stated:

> The parent group called, just to let me know they were around. When I was ready, I called them. I am again pregnant, so I have a list of mothers who have already experienced their subsequent children's births. Just talking to someone who has been there often eases my unfounded fears for my unborn baby.

> My neighbor lost a baby to SIDS in Tennessee four years ago. She cried with me when I found Timmy. She stripped my bed where he was found, and cleared all the dirty baby things out of the house so that I would not have to wash them. She kept them at her house until I was ready to cope with putting them away.

> Our minister cried with us as he prayed for Timmy, and explained to us that though he had not been baptized, he was pure and entered heaven.

> Our family doctor called every day for the first week to see how we were getting along. He was almost as hurt as we were.

This woman experienced a tremendous amount of support that will help both her and her family put the pieces back together again. Others are not so lucky, as a Kansas woman related: "All of our parents and others refused to accept that such a syndrome could exist and insisted our baby died of pneumonia. Some friends did not know how to react to us or what to say and flatly stayed away from all contact. One girl did not want me to go near her baby. We lost some friendships during this time."

It is difficult, if not impossible, to expect a family to understand if we try to isolate them and pull away support at just the time they will need it the most. We must let the family set the limits for the amount of support they need, as one mother in Montana wrote eight weeks after the death of her sixteen-week-old son, "Sometimes I get the feeling people wish I would get over mourning soon, but I still feel like talking about Josh and it makes people uncomfortable."

Families, instead of coming together and offering each other strength, often can create situations that may have long-term effects on the bereaved parents. One Montana woman told us: "Some of my in-laws questioned how our names as parents were put on his gravestone. My name was put on before my husband's. His relatives thought it should have been the opposite way. We weren't thinking of the order of names at the time, we were upset.

But after they mentioned it we were both upset to think of what they cared about most—our names, not his death.''

Professionals can also make decisions that profoundly affect the parents of the child. One mother from North Dakota shared this with us after the death of her daughter:

> The physician who pronounced our baby dead told us she died of "aspiration" (also on the death certificate), which implied guilt on our part, or a preventable death. He told my father-in-law, as an aside, that it could be a "crib death," but never mentioned that to us.
>
> The biggest setback in my grieving process occurred about three months after the death. A student nurse, also a neighbor and friend, who was with us during the labor and delivery and postpartum check-ups, told us that she and a pediatric nurse practitioner (who had never met us) thought we were mourning "abnormally." We had written an article for the air-base paper six to eight weeks after her death; I guess the nurse thought parents should or could do that ten years later. It was therapy for us, though. Anyway, I tried to talk to this "friend," but only ended in anger, tears, and self-doubt. Was I "abnormal," indeed? I have considered her behavior a betrayal of my trust and friendship, and still regard her with anger and bitterness. My husband helped me to put these women's opinions in the proper perspective after a few weeks of many tears and much introspection.

Who sets the boundaries and defines a normal grief process? This can be done only by the individuals who are involved in the loss. Trite cliches such as "time heals" can bring fourth a response of anger, much to the surprise of the well-intended individual. One woman shared with us that if one more person told her that time heals she was going to "punch her out." In retrospect she can see that the passage of time does indeed help; but in the midst of her shock and grief it was incomprehensible.

There are attitudes and feelings that people who have lost a child share with others, and it is in a sense reassuring to these people that this too shall pass. In a broadly defined manner, it is helpful to inform families that what they are experiencing has been similar to the experiences of others. For those in a helping profession, it is important to stress the commonality shared by families during such a crisis. Margaret Pomeroy and Bruce Beckwith, associated with the National Foundation for Sudden Infant Death, have found that these can be simple statements, such as, "You will have emotional ups and downs."[2] There is no prediction of when this will happen or prevention for it happening. SIDS parents will have to tell themselves this over and over again until they believe it. Insomnia complaints and bad dreams are common, as well as somatic complaints (headaches, stomach ache, back pain, and so forth). Accepting the reality of the situation takes time, and it is common to continue to get up at night to check the baby, prepare the bath, and fix the baby's food for some time after the death. It is also common not to want to be left alone, especially for mothers who find it disturbing to be left alone in the same house or apartment where the baby died. Many parents complain of feeling that they were "going crazy" because they could not concentrate or do routine tasks that they had done all of their lives. Loss of appetite can be another aspect of the inner turmoil parents are experiencing.

Beckwith and Pomeroy also found that the parents, rather than outwardly clinging to the remaining children, may be irritated by their behavior. The tolerance level for the children's normal behavior may be very low. At the same time, they may feel overly concerned for their safety and may want to escape the weight of responsibility for them. Well-meaning, helpful friends and relatives may be irritating, which often leaves the parents feeling guilty again for resenting those who are trying to help.

Knowledge of common experiences and understanding that each individual deals with grief in a unique way can lend support and reassurance to the family that they are okay. Still, even saying the right thing at the right time will not make the pain any less. We speak in terms of easing pain or alleviating guilt, when basically we are feeling very helpless at not being able to physically take from these suffering families a measure of their pain. Of course, no one can.

An expression of understanding in a nonverbal manner can convey a powerful message of caring. One young mother from Connecticut experienced such empathy:

> Our son was not taken from us. My husband and I accompanied him into the examining room. We were allowed to remain there afterwards. My father joined us and we were given assistance in contacting our minister and the funeral director. Everyone was kind and sympathetic, no hospital bureaucracy (and later no bill).

> Friends, relatives, and professional people need to realize parents be allowed choices. They (the parents) must later live with the decisions, right or wrong; they must be given several opportunities to change their minds, as our funeral director did. On three occasions he gave us the opportunity to see our son again, though each time we refused. No pressure, just understanding.

At times, effects to reduce the pain miss the mark. It is difficult if not impossible for parents to believe their baby is "better off where he is," and "that he has been saved from living in this cruel world."

Attempts to remove from view signs of the baby can be met with resistance and should only be done with permission. Do not do the family a favor by packing up the child's things without talking to them first. One woman from a small town in Missouri expressed these feelings:

> My mother and close friend took everthing down and put Josh's clothes and toys out of sight. So I came home to an empty house after viewing my dead baby.

Most of the time it is what people say: "You have three beautiful children," "At least you have her twin," "I check my children every night so they won't die of SIDS," "How could you want another baby? Do you want to go through that again?"

Seemingly small things can upset and irritate:

One thing that hurt terribly was when we received a sympathy card from one of my relatives. She stated "I was so sorry to hear about the loss of your baby, I never even got to see it." She knew darn well Timmy was a boy and had a name. Just the use of that pronoun upset me.

Friends, relatives, and professionals interested in helping parents deal with the loss might be advised to allow the parents to mourn in their own way, and let them know that help is available when they need it. Parents need the factual information that is available about SIDS to help alleviate the guilt they may feel over the death. Knowing that their reactions to the loss are not abnormal and that other parents have had similar experiences can be of comfort and help parents realize that they are not "going crazy."

Notes

1. The nurse's visit to SIDS families, Nebraska SIDS Project, 1980, p. 1.

2. B. Beckwith, *The Sudden Infant Death Syndrome.* DHEW Publication no. HSA 75–5137 (U.S. Government Printing Office, 1978).

**What Do I Tell
the Other Children?**

When we think of the death of a child, we usually tend to think of it in terms of a mother's loss. Yet as we pointed out, fathers suffer also; they might not suffer as visibly, but still the death is a crisis for fathers. In this chapter we will look at how the children in the family, siblings of the dead infant, are affected.

In our culture children are sheltered from pain and suffering. Our eagerness to protect children, however, can lead to an unbearably stressful situation when a death occurs in the family. It is tempting to avoid confronting the other children with the death of their baby brother or sister, because the initial shock creates a sense of numbness and loss of reality for the parents, and it is at first difficult for parents to come to terms with their own feelings. One father from California related these kinds of feelings to us:

> When we attended the first SIDS meeting, we all told our stories and we discovered we were the only ones who had lost their first child. I thought how much easier it was for them, they had other children to fill the silence. Our apartment was so lonely.
>
> But as we talked I began to realize how difficult it is to explain to a young child why the baby died when I couldn't understand why a baby has to die myself.

What do we tell the children? How much should they know? What will they understand? These questions confront parents at a very vulnerable time, a time when they feel inadequate to deal with their own feelings, let alone a child's.

To understand a child's experience, it is necessary to remember that today most children are continuously prepared for the birth of a new child into the family. They are told what Mom and Dad will do to care for the new baby and how they will be able to help. In an effort to avoid sibling rivalry and ready the family for a new member, we help children rehearse for their new role as older brother or sister. Usually this will include expectations that the child will be more grown-up; and with the new status will also come certain privileges that the younger infant will not be entitled to.

Family life is just settling down to a new routine when tragedy occurs, and for the child the world is turned upside down.

The first question in a child's mind is usually, "What happened?" On giving explanations it is important to use correct terms. The statement can be simply that the baby, by name, has died and will not be returning to the home. The child should be told that the death of the baby was a result of a physical failure of the infant's body. To a very young child these words might be only, "Kim's body quit breathing and her heart stopped beating. It didn't start again and she is dead." Along with this explanation the parents should reassure the child that she or he is big and strong and will not die like the baby. Children ages two to five will be particularly concerned about the adequacy of their own bodies.[1]

One of the next questions might be, "Why did the baby not live?" This will be most difficult, because no one knows for sure why babies die from SIDS. This can be an important part of the explanation, and it need not be frightening for the child to know that the parents cannot explain the why of this loss. The lack of an explanation can become part of the reality of the event. That is to say that parents are neither perfect nor omnipotent, and there are things that they cannot control or explain. "I don't know why she died. No one knows."[2]

Religious explanation can be comforting for some children and frightening for others. One child may be satisfied with "God wanted the baby with him." But another child, often in the same family, will wonder why God chose the baby and not her? Will she be next? These fears will not always be verbalized specifically by the child, and the parents must be alert to signals the child may be giving. This could be a preoccupation with questions about God: Where is He? How does He stay up there? How does He decide who to take with Him?

As adults, our own sense of permanence is shattered by the sudden, unexpected death of an infant. We must realize that a child's thinking is not nearly as complex, and his or her concept of how the world is organized rests on tenuous threads.

Harriet Sarnoff Schiff makes this point about "magical thinking" in her book, *The Bereaved Parent*. "As children many of us are taught to pray or wish for things we want, and if we are good our wishes just may come true. It we're good, Santa Claus will come down from the North Pole and heap gifts upon us. The Tooth Fairy's going to stash money under our pillow, and Cinderella's fairy godmother just might also be ours, to. "Pray to God and if you are very good He will answer your prayers."[3] Wishing for children is often rewarded, and very young children often cannot separate out that wishing does not necessarily make it so. Billy Graham was once asked the question, "Does God answer all prayers?" He replied; "Yes He does, but sometimes the answer is no." This concept is very hard for children to understand. Therefore, they must be reassured that their thoughts are not actions and wishes do not always come true.

Most children have been told that people do not die until they are very old. The child might have already experienced this with the death of a grandparent. A clear contradiction occurs with the death of an infant, and this undermines the child's confidence in adult pronouncements. Children will try to solve this problem by placing the death of the child in concrete terms, such as: "You die because you're small"; "You die young only at night"; "Only girls die"; and the like. Still, the reality of the situation cannot be avoided, and as parents must confront their own thoughts and fears, so must the child. Simple, direct answers should be adequate. They can be elaborated on if necessary when the child is older, and yet they should be honest enough to satisfy the child. They will probably have to be repeated many times, so be prepared. As the parents go over and over the death, so do the surviving children.

Sickness, like old age, appears on the surface to be a simple way to deal with a child's questions of why. Yet children will combine, in what may seem to adults a bizarre fashion, old parental urgings about sleep, food, and sickness. Warnings about running around barefoot, "You'll catch your death of cold," or "Eat your vegetables so you'll grow up nice and strong," can be converted into reasons the baby died; and the child will often worry needlessly that he will become sick and die also. This is not to say that parents should guard against ever uttering a cliche, but during an emotionally charged time such as this is, many explanations might be necessary for what parents could consider trivial questions. Again it is important to reassure the child that his body is strong. And as parents who are experiencing fear, guilt, and anger, it is essential that the child be allowed to express similar feelings. Children feel the same things as adults, but they simply think differently.

"God took the baby to be with Him in heaven" is another common explanation given to children that comforts some parents as well as some children. But this can lead to confusion about God's portrayal as benevolent. Children are puzzled as to how and why their loved and loving God would kill or, at best, take away their sibling. Some need constant reassurance that God does not really go around hurting people.[4]

Some parents choose not to talk about God at all with their children and argue that it makes more sense in a time of death or crisis simply to say: "I just don't know why." These parents feel that questions about God are essentially unanswerable and to get into discussions of heaven, hell, and other theological issues is harmful or confusing to children. These parents tend to believe that God is a human invention to mask fear of the unknown. "My role as a parent is to help my child learn to think and to adapt to the world's problems. I'm not going to fill my kid's head full of superstition that doesn't help him,'' one mother argued. Other parents, of course, would be horrified by such an approach.

Parental overprotectiveness of the remaining children is a typical response to the loss of a child. These feelings can be examined, and it must be acknowledged that as parents you might never feel quite the same confidence that your children live in an orderly, predictable, safe world. Simultaneously, you must build up strength and confidence that as parents you have done and will do all that is necessary to assure safety for your children. At first, it will be a fine line, one that is open to criticism, but it must be remembered that the child might also be suffering from feelings of vulnerability in a world where notions of her parents' invulnerability and strength as protectors are at odds with reality. The sharing of confusion and helplessness with the children will not be as traumatic for them as their fears of the unknown. The illusion that all is well when the child will invariably sense that it just isn't so can leave the family isolated and fragmented. Conversations that cease when the child enters the room will not go unnoticed and could create misinformation that later will be hard to correct.

The young preschool child is experiencing thought processes in which the difference between feelings and causing events in reality is confused. A child, who has felt anger at the baby for taking up so much of Mom and Dad's time and wished the baby were gone, might harbor some guilt that his wish has come true. These feelings can be worked through if the parents will remember that they also harbor guilt feelings about the times they wished the baby would sleep longer or the times they let the baby cry. The parents can share with the child these feelings and point out that nothing the parent or the child did or thought caused the death of the baby.

Some parents say that almost from birth one child is more closely identified with one parent than the other. Parents on occasion state that ''He was always my husband's baby.'' If it is ''your'' baby that died, chances are that you will experience some resentment toward the other child or children. One mother said, ''Why is my baby dead and his (my husband's) still alive?'' It was not easy for her to admit these feelings and openly talk to her husband about them; but once out in the open, the act of sharing enabled her to work through resentments she felt.

Parents can help children deal with the loss of a baby brother or sister by realistically indicating what happened to the deceased child. These answers will depend on the age of the child, but even a very young child is going to organize in her mind some explanation of why death occurred without parental help. It is best not to give the child explanations that you do not personally believe in; the inconsistency will eventually surface causing the child further anxiety, uncertainty, and skepticism. It is essential to reassure the child that her feelings were not a factor in the death of the infant and that all people have similar feelings at times.

The child also is having to deal with parental grief. Although having experienced a loss, the young child will not experience the grief with the same intensity as his parents and acceptance of this by the parents will help let them respond to the child that they do not expect the child to feel the same way they do. This leads to the question of whether the child should attend the funeral or visit the funeral home. This again should depend on the age of the child and family custom. The ceremony and ritual of the funeral can encourage feelings of acceptance of the death and give the family a sense of closure. The rigid rules of many funerals can make decisions easier for the parents; and if one of the rules is that children attend funerals, the parents need not agonize over how this will effect the other children. Older children can be asked if they wish to attend, and their wishes should be accepted by other family members. Some children will appear to mourn deeply, while others are seemingly untouched by the death. Value judgments as to the depth of the child's feeling should be avoided. Older children might request a greater amount of participation in making arrangements and should be included in such discussions. The parents' judgment about their children should be respected; well-meaning relatives probably do not know any better than the parents do.

The anger and frustration that appears as the mourning process continues can be confusing to a child. But this can be minimized if the parents can say to the child, "We are angry because we wanted a baby, and now we don't have one." This can be easily understood by even young children, and they will realize that they are not the cause of the anger.

Most of the parents in our study emphasized that the one thing to anger them the most is people who try to ignore the existence of the baby. And yet, because of the surviving child's young age or obvious distress at the mention of the baby, parents may avoid talking about the baby in front of the child. But the child is grieving also and should be allowed to participate with the parents in recalling events or memories of the dead child. Feelings of loss, grief, anger, and disappointment, and permission for the family to talk about them will help the child accept these feelings.

Children's ideas about death are different at different age levels. Even very young children are interested in finding out more about the subject. This is also true in the event of sudden, unexpected death when there is no time for preparation. The best explanations for children, especially those under age seven or eight, will be those that are simple and direct, and draw as much as possible from the child's own experience.[5]

It is always useful when explaining death to a child to have the child explain back what he has been told. This will allow for any misunderstandings to be straightened out immediately before fears of the child distort what he has been told. Keep in mind that Jean Piaget's research has found that young children, ages seven and below, might not believe or be able to conceptualize that death is permanent.[6] Questions about the baby's return might persist for some time. A simple "No, the baby will never return" is usually sufficient; but it will probably lead to questions about where the baby is. If the child has been told that the baby is in heaven with God, frequent visits to the grave will necessitate further explanation. "If the baby is in heaven, then why was she placed in the ground?" One way to handle such inquiries is to assure the child that the grave is merely a remembrance of the child. For the very young child it will be difficult for her to understand that life has left the body and only the body remains. That, of course is most difficult for adults to understand, also. Where did life go?

Silence can build walls in a family when individuals most need support and strength for each other. Even young children can show support and help to solidify the family when death occurs.[7] All children need to feel a part of what is happening and must find their own level of involvement and degree of mourning. To share sadness and grief with the children reaffirms that they are truly members of a family and that we can trust them with our feelings. They in turn will come to realize that while we are not omnipotent as parents, we can offer them a safe refuge in which to grow and discover thoughts and emotions without censor.

Notes

1. O.L. Weston, and R.C. Irwin, "Preschool Child's Response to the Death of Infant Sibling," *American Journal of Diseases of Children* 106 (1963):564–567.

2. H.S. Schiff, *The Bereaved Parent* (New York: Crown Publisher, 1977), p. 38.

3. Ibid.

4. A.C. Cain, I. Fast, and M.E. Erickson, "Children's Disturbed Reactions to the Death of a Sibling," *American Journal of Orthopsychiatry,* 34 (1964):741–752.

5. G.P. Koocher, "Talking with Children about Death," *American Journal of Orthopsychiatry,* 44 (1964):404–411.

6. J. Piaget, *The Child's Conception of the World* (New Jersey: Littlefield, Adams and Co., 1960).

7. C. Hargrove, and L. Warrich, "How Shall We Tell the Children?" *American Journal of Nursing,* 74 (1974):448–450.

9

Can It Happen Again?
On Having Another Baby

The decision whether to have another baby is perhaps the most difficult one that families have to face. The parents might have feelings of incompetence and question their ability as parents. They wonder if the family could survive another crisis. One Indiana mother explained her feelings: "I have felt guilt, I was afraid to have any more children. I thought people would think I wasn't a good mother because the baby died. When I would see another baby it would hurt. Then one-and-a-half years later I had twins and that more than anything seemed to help both my husband and me forget."

There appears to be a pattern of thought that many parents go through when deciding to have another baby. After the initial shock of losing their baby, they often feel angry and report that they said or felt they would never have another baby. The very idea of replacing an infant that brought them so much joy is repugnant. You do not just replace a baby the way you would a car. One young mother shared her thoughts:

> At first I thought if I couldn't have my baby back I didn't ever want another baby. I felt cheated, why couldn't it have been one of the other women in town with new babies? We were so proud of Brian; my husband got to see him born. But I remember all the special moments and they make me happy and help me get through the bad times. I'm doing babysitting now and that helps. I'm expecting another baby now and this has helped me a lot. I'm going to be afraid for awhile when the baby goes to sleep, but that will be something I'll just have to get through.—a New York mother

Time is part of the process of coming to a decision to have a subsequent child, but the length of time can be as varied as are the individuals involved. One mother from Nebraska shared with us that she was angry the day she and her husband found their infant dead; but three days later she decided she wanted another child and became pregnant almost immediately. It is not unusual for families to wait several years before they come to the decision to have another baby; some decide never to have any more children.

Attitude, more than the time element, seems to be a factor when deciding to have another child. When the family once again finds life going on and can rejoin the mainstream, then a decision can be made. Still the terror that it could happen again is not dispelled, regardless of the length of time. The pregnancy can be a time of anxious moments, and the birth of the child a time of panic.

Can it happen again? While it is impossible to answer that question with an unqualified no, the statistics give relative comfort. Parents have to remind themselves that if only one out of every 350 babies die of SIDS, then certainly 349 live.[1] But even such heartening statistics cannot remove the fear.

> I got pregnant almost immediately with my daughter, who is now four years old. I was terrified that the same thing would happen again. I spent the first year of my daughter's life in fear. It was horrible. I was fine during the day, even though I checked her breathing constantly. But in the evening I was restless. Our son died during the night and I had to live with the fear of the same thing reoccuring. I checked my baby daughter several times each night for at least six months. I don't remember resting peacefully until she was about two years old. It was the only way I could cope, and I know I would do it again if I had to for peace of mind.—an Indiana mother

After the birth of the baby there is a flood of emotions. Baby clothes serve as reminders of the lost baby. Perhaps the same baby bed is used. And always the thought, "How will I ever sleep through the night?" For awhile, perhaps you will not. Parents often feel a sense of panic. Carolyn Szybist defines panic so well: it is freezing at the door to the infant's room, afraid to enter because something certainly must be wrong; it is awakening in the middle of the night and breaking into a cold sweat while someone else has to go and check to see if the baby is all right; it is being certain the baby is not breathing and shaking him until a sleepy two-month-old looks up wondering what is going on. Panic teaches you the lesson that your greatest fear is not for the infant, but for yourself: "Your concern is how you would survive emotionally if you lost this child too."[2]

And yet all the advice in the world cannot negate your fears and you strive to live as best you can. Considering the circumstances, most of the families come through the decision to have another baby successfully, but it can take a long time.

The question of monitoring can arise when a decision is made to have another baby. There is much controversy surrounding the use of home monitors. Physically the monitor is quite simple: electrodes are placed on the baby's diaphragm. This monitors the baby's breathing and will signal with an alarm if the baby ceases to breathe for longer than twenty seconds. Some families who have experienced a death from SIDS have decided to place subsequent children on a home monitor, but it must be pointed out that researchers have not definitively proven that apnea or cessation of breathing is the single cause of SIDS. One parent told us that she responded to the monitor, only to find that the infant had disconnected the electrode and was clutching it in her fist. This, of course, caused some very anxious moments. The stress can affect family relationships, and there is no 100 percent guarantee that an infant will still not succumb to SIDS, even while on the monitor. The advantages as well as the risks must be weighed. Some parents felt they could not sleep at all without a monitor; it gave them a sense of security and was a positive experience for the family. The psychological advantages of the home monitor appear to be very important.

In a study of thirty-five infants that had been identified as at high risk for apneatic episodes, four deaths occurred despite monitoring.[3] A research team at the Children's Hospital Medical Center and Boston Hospital for Women argued that even if those with severe apneatic episodes could be diagnosed and placed on twenty-four-hour surveillance by caregivers skilled in cardiopulmonary resuscitation, and even if this surveillance were 100 percent effective, it would affect only a small proportion of infants at risk for SIDS. They estimated that only 5 percent of SIDS victims have a history of prolonged apnea; the majority of deaths are unexpected.[4]

Many communities are too small to have the resources for monitoring, and many parents are too financially burdened to attempt to carry out a home-monitoring program. The decision to have a subsequent child is up to the families involved, and well-intentioned friends should not encourage or discourage what is ultimately decided.

There is no guarantee that the birth of a subsequent child will speed the process of working through the grief of losing the other baby. But some parents stated that it did indeed help them to recover. Others, although they would never give up their subsequent children, have told of many anxious moments until the child had reached what for the parents was the safe age. Many, many families can and do go on to have other children and have found the strength to survive and find happiness once again as a family.

Notes

1. C. Szybist, *The Subsequent Child.* DHEW Publication no. HSA 78-5260 (U.S. Government Printing Office, 1978).

2. Ibid.

3. N. Nelson, "But Who Shall Monitor the Monitor?" *Pediatrics* 61 (1978):663-664.

4. A. Stark, F. Mandell, and H. Taeusch, "Close Encounters with SIDS," *Pediatrics* (1978):61 664-665.

10 How Do Families Survive?

Parents who experience the sudden, unexpected death of an infant are often young. They have waited with anticipation for nine months for the birth of their child. This anticipation is often a mix of happiness, confusion, and fear. The entry of the new baby into the home causes a considerable degree of stress, but adjustments gradually are made and life has often resumed a more normal pattern when without warning the baby dies. Quite often this is the couple's first experience with death.

According to Stanley Weinstein, "a common denominator in SIDS parents is guilt." Guilt, grief, and lack of knowledge about SIDS taken together become a major emotional stress for parents, both as individuals and as a couple. The guilt can exacerbate previous emotional problems and marital difficulties. "The grief and mourning are doubly hard because the parents had no preparation—the infants were viewed as thriving and healthy, not sickly."[1]

In our initial study of SIDS families it was found that 50 percent of the parents who had experienced SIDS in the state of Nebraska could not be found for participation in the research; within six months to two-and-a-half years after the death, half of the parents moved from their hometowns, leaving no forwarding address. This high rate of mobility might be an indication that these parents possibly felt that only by leaving their homes and hometowns could they forget or recover from the death.[2] It might also indicate that early participation with a parent support group is needed to promote a feeling a belonging and lessen the isolation these families might have felt.

Just when a couple may need each other the most, they may be most vulnerable and unable to help each other. Anne Morrow Lindbergh in her book *Dearly Beloved* wrote, "Grief can't be shared. Everyone carries it alone, his own burden, his own way."[3] The death of a baby happens to both the mother and the father; yet, their experiences with grief and mourning may be totally different, and their approaches to coping may go in opposite directions. Sharing becomes difficult when a parent is in so much pain that to survive each day can become a selfish endeavor. For the individual it is a matter of rigid concentration, and a person's thoughts are narrowed to just getting out of bed, just getting dressed, just getting through one more day.

This can take all of the individual's energy and it is difficult to have any left to share with the spouse.

Angry feelings that husbands and wives have for each other are difficult to deny. Each person will have their own notions about how grief should be displayed and these will not be the same for any two individuals. Tension may result when the wife feels the husband is having too good a time; or he may become resentful when she wants to make love. "How could anyone think of sex at a time like this?" he may think, revolted.

These feelings can create a separateness at a time when relatives and friends are leaving the family alone to mourn. A person is truly alone then, when the mate who is counted on cannot understand one's feelings. Any relationship will experience times of stress, but the loss of an infant represents a time of crisis that is individually devastating and can be totally destructive to a marriage.

Parents who have lost a child can find themselves suddenly out of control. A feeling of powerlessness pervades the relationship as parents discover that they were unable to protect their child; they feel impotent because they must come to terms with the fact that they have no control over whether or not a child lives or dies.

Shared adversity often builds bonds between people; but the sharing of the loss of a child will not necessarily create a stronger bond between a husband and wife. Grief and the process of mourning is a series of small steps taken when the individual is ready, and the marriage often takes second place to individual recovery.

The very different nature of parenthood for men and women creates a different experience for them. Young mothers are bound to have "conflicted feelings about the helpless infant and worry about their maternal adequacy," according to Werner Halpern. The sudden death of a baby "lays bare these ambivalent feelings and doubts." Fathers, on the other hand, are usually less involved in infant care and so "are not as vulnerable to the psychic hazard of questionning their role in sudden infant death."[4]

Mothers, being concerned with the day-to-day care of the infant, may feel a tremendous loss of purpose in life. Bath time, feeding time, nap time can all become empty hours that must be filled. Fathers may feel deep remorse that they had not spent more time with the child instead of looking toward the future when the child would be old enough to teach and share his skills.

One mother explained how it was for her and her husband:

> After we had Matthew our worlds were complete. We had a beautiful daughter and a beautiful son. We had the happiest and most fulfilled life we had ever had. Then Matthew died and it felt like our world had been crushed and taken away.
>
> I fell apart at first and Rick was strong for me. Then about three months later I started getting better and Rick started to fall apart.

To put it bluntly, I feel I have been terribly beaten and weakened in some way that I know I will never be the same again. It's true that nothing or no one can ever take the place of the loved one you've lost, no matter how hard you may try. There will always be a terrible empty void that nothing will fill.

Every month that went by I would always think Matt would have been so many months old.

Every holiday, happy and yet unhappy because he will not be there to share it.

The day which would have been his first birthday was very hard.

Sometimes it is hard not to still feel bitterness, but that gets you nowhere, so pick up and start again.

It hurts me very much because the son we wanted so badly is gone and we miss him terribly.

If I see other boys his age I ache, for I will never know what he would have looked like.

He was such a beautiful baby and touched so many people's lives in ways some people who live to be one hundred don't even accomplish. He filled us with love and warmth and we have many loving memories of him to cherish forever.

I feel very lost and empty a lot of the time. It can be very easy for me to feel sorry for myself. "WHY ME?" Everyone thinks it happens to everyone else until it hits home.

I feel I've gone through so much, sometimes I thought I'd never pull through, but I did and I seem to be stronger for it.—an Iowa mother

Families can and do cope and are successful with dealing with the crisis of sudden infant death. In research on how strong families cope with crisis, investigators Nick Stinnett, Barbara Knorr, John DeFrain, and George Rowe found that one major factor in coping is the support an individual receives from the family, and positive growth can occur despite the initial disorganization that comes with crisis.[5]

As John DeFrain is fond of saying to his students, "Two of the best kept-secrets in the Twentieth Century are: Everyone suffers, and suffering can be used for growing and becoming."

A mother in Pennsylvania who responded to our study explained how it was for her: "I have endured the closest thing to hell on earth that could possibly be able to happen. I have found compassion and understanding from perfect strangers, yet cold and heartless emotions from close friends and relatives. All in all it has been a growing process. I found personal strength and power from within which I never knew existed or had ever tapped."

How can one family find ways to cope with the death of a child, while another may be torn apart? Individually, all members of a family may adjust to and learn to live with the death of an infant, and yet some do not make it as families. There is no simple answer, but a multiplicity of factors can enhance the family's chances of survival and perhaps move them in a positive direction after the death of an infant.

Communication, of course, is of utmost importance to the process of adjustment to the crisis. When an infant dies suddenly, the guilt and anger may cause a wall of silence to be erected within a family. The placing of blame may prevent couples from communicating. A slammed door, a drunken spouse, or a mother so numb with grief that the thought of sex with her husband is repellent—all can destroy any kind of adequate environment for effective communication.

Effective communication includes sharing, not only between spouses, but with friends and relatives. Finding strength within the family and using it as a resource is important to coping, and when this does not happen the results can affect the individual for a long time:

> Thirty-seven years have passed, and until four years ago I was not allowed to talk about it. Not to my husband or family or friends. It was only with my daughter's neighbor, who had gone through the same experience, just recently that I was finally allowed to talk and receive some comfort. No one knew thirty-seven years ago that SIDS existed, and all I knew was what the doctor said: "Suffocation." Not another word.—a Missouri mother

The research on strong families reported by Stinnett, Knorr, DeFrain, and Rowe found that many of the families were reliant on God to help them through crisis experiences.[6] Many individuals experiencing a death from SIDS also said that their belief in God was helpful and that being able to tell themselves that their baby was with God was one of the few comforts they received. Other individuals cautioned that reliance on God was not all they did to recover from crisis. A father from Nebraska expressed it this way: "Optimism that things will work out for the best, or faith in God's will, is important. But you've got to actively try to help yourself. You can't sit back and wait for God to help. You've got to get out of your rut yourself."

Commitment, togetherness, and the ability to take turns being strong for each other were also seen as positive ways with which to cope with the loss of a child. Affection and communication can bring strength into a crisis situation.

A final common denominator appears to be an individual's simple ability to survive—to get up in the morning and get through the day, to force concentration on tasks that may seem irrelevant to the situation. One woman found herself thinking, "How can I scrub this floor? My baby is dead." But she knew she had to keep busy and involved, if even on such a basic level.

For these parents some measure of control over their lives is returned to them as they realize that they are going to survive the loss, the pain will diminish and they are stronger for it. "There is always a way out. No problem is insoluble. The resources of the human spirit to meet and triumph over adversity have amazed me again and again. There seems to be almost nothing men and women cannot do when they are wholly resolved upon it," as stated in David R. Mace's book.[7]

Many parents expressed surprise that they did survive the death of their baby. Once the realization had sunk in that they would live though their baby did not live, they found strength in themselves they never thought possible before. Most of them grimly acknowledged the truth of one Illinois mother's words: "Now I can survive anything."

Notes

1. S. Weinstein, "Sudden Infant Death Syndrome: Impact on Families and a Direction for Change," *American Journal of Psychiatry* 137 (1978):7.

2. J. DeFrain, and L. Ernst, "The Psychological Effects of Sudden Infant Death Syndrome on Surviving Family Members," *Journal of Family Practice* 6 (1978):985–989.

3. A.M. Lindbergh, *Dearly Beloved* (New York: Harcourt, Brace and World, 1962).

4. W. Halpern, "Some Psychiatric Sequelae to Crib Death," *American Journal of Psychiatry* (1972):129.

5. N. Stinnett, B. Knorr, J. DeFrain, and G. Rowe, "How Strong Families Cope with Crises," *Family Perspective* (Fall 1981).

6. Ibid.

7. D.R. Mace, *Success in Marriage* (Nashville: Abingdon Press, 1958).

11 Support for Parents Who Have Lost Babies to SIDS

Clar Nelson and *Jan Stork*

Both women who contributed to this chapter have lost babies. It is essential to recognize that those parents who have experienced the tragic loss of an infant offer an invaluable resource and depth of understanding for others who will face such a death in the future.

Our experience as researchers is a vicarious one; we can only imagine what it must feel like to have a baby die. We shed tears, and yet they are tears for the pain we have seen in these families who were courageous enough to participate in this study.

This chapter is written by two women whose first-hand experiences have led them into an involvement with bereaved parents they would have never believed possible. Clar and Scott Nelson of Waverly, Nebraska, lost a son four months of age to SIDS. Since then they have both been active in working for legislation to insure that a systematic and immediate protocol is followed in all cases of suspected SIDS. Clar is also available to parents when a SIDS death occurs. Clar talks here about the experience.

The day had been a good one: things seem to fall into place well and the children have not really dealt me too many problems. The phone rings. It is the Nurse's Association informing me a baby died last night: three-and-a-half-months old, a baby girl, preliminary autopsy reports probably SIDS.

My pulse races as she gives me the details and background on the baby and parents. I say a silent prayer as I continue to write down the information. The nurse tells me the parents are anxious to visit with a parent who has experienced this crisis.

The conversation ends and my mind starts to fill full of memories of that awful day in December. What was said to me to help the hurt? What helped to take away my guilt? What things enabled Scott and me to get to where we are today?

I have to help these people, can I do it? Will they want help, or will they turn me away? Questions! Questions! They don't stop until the door opens and those pain-filled eyes meet mine. Immediately, there is a bond; our babies have died, suddenly and without warning. There are so many feelings: guilt, fear, loneliness, hate, confusion, on and on. All of these must be shared.

Shared is the key word. What Scott and I do is not counsel, but share with and listen to these people. Neither of us are qualified to do counseling, but we are terrific listeners.

Parents who experience this kind of crisis often need to talk about their experiences, but find this hard to do. Somehow if you know the person that you are visiting with has felt those same feelings and saw the same awful sight of a dead baby (your own baby) it makes it a little easier to open up and release some of those harbored feelings.

When David died, Scott and I had no one to talk to about his death; there was no one who had gone through the same hell we had. Many times I had thought if only I could tell someone how awful he looked when we found him and have the person know that same feeling. I needed to share all those ugly feelings and I needed to share them with someone who had felt the same things.

Soon after David's death I had decided I wanted to help people deal with and work through the death of their baby.

Nebraska had a bill introduced to its legislature in 1979 stating there would be mandatory autopsies funded by the state and that the state would provide some form of counseling for the parents. The bill passed, and the counseling was left up to each county as to how it would be handled. Scott and I attended the hearing and there met Len Ormsby, who's baby had died of SIDS a year before. I later met Len's wife, Chris.

Chris and I soon found a mutual bond not only in that we had both lost babies to SIDS, but we had a concern of how the counseling was being handled in our county. With every ounce of courage we had, we met with our county attorney. Our purpose was to set up a specific protocol to be used in all SIDS deaths. He was very receptive and accepted all of our ideas. From that meeting our system was set up.

Once a death has been designated as SIDS, the coroner notifies a nursing facility. A nurse then makes an initial visit within forty-eight hours of the death. She relays all the medical information available. The nurse then contacts a SIDS parent who is willing to make personal contacts with these families in crisis. We try to make contact by phone immediately and hopefully visit personally within two weeks.

The nurse makes two return visits. We try to keep frequent contact with these parents for as long as they need us. We now have a group of parents that get together for coffees, picnics, films, and other social events. The group shares and tries to work through various problems that arise.

I have two main goals when I visit these parents. One, to get them to open up and talk about what they are feeling, what they saw, what other people said to them, the confusion over what SIDS is, and what is the hardest thing they are trying to deal with about the death of their baby. The second goal I try to accomplish is to help them rid themselves of any guilt feelings they may be having.

Many of us want to bottle up all those feelings in hopes they will go away, but vanish they do not; they only build to become greater. If we can share them with someone, somehow it helps them to heal. The hurt will never disappear completely, but it will lessen if we deal with it.

Every visit I make brings back memories of that first day when a mother who I had never met before put her arms around me and said, "Thank you for understanding." It makes that hurt meaningful.

I often share a poem I have written with these parents whose babies have died, and now I would like to share it with you.

Our Joy

He was given to us
   so tiny,
   so helpless.
In five short months
   no longer
   was his dependency on us
   but we on him.
He gave us smiles,
   when all was down.
Showed us that two a.m.
   was a delightful time of day.
Giggled at brother's antics
   when no one else did.
And he never tired of being happy.

The morning was bright, sunny,
   and so alive with joy.
The brightness of his eyes
   did not glitter with affection.
The sunny smile was wiped away.
The joy he brought to each day . . . was gone.

God gives all a duty.
David did his well.
He gave so much, and took only love in return.
Thank you God for your gift of David.
Thank you God for returning him to Your arms,
   for he was our joy
   and now the joy is his, forever.

I really can not give you an easy formula for forming a parents support group. The first thing I would suggest is to contact: National Sudden Infant Death Syndrome Foundation; 2 Metro Plaza, Suite 205; 8240 Professional Place; Landover, Maryland 20785. You might ask the foundation for information concerning parent groups in your area. Some states have very good state foundations set up and some are not as well organized, so you may find a need to start your own group. Again, the national foundation may be of help in giving you some names to get started.

The laws vary from state to state as to what kind of information they can give you about the families of SIDS victims, but you might try contacting your state health department.

Do not neglect those parents who have lost children to other causes, particularly if you are in a sparsely populated area. We who have experienced the death of a child all feel loss, guilt, and emptiness; the cause of death is the only difference. Trying to start a parents' group may be slow and very discouraging at times, but do not give up, for the rewards and the help you will be able to give the bereaved parent will be endless.

Jan and Warren Stork, also of Lincoln, Nebraska, were instrumental in setting up the Infant Crisis Parent League. Jan talks about why:

Our twins were born 30 September 1976. They were due to be born 15 December 1976, thus they had come two and one-half months early. Nathan, who was first born, weighed in at two pounds, three ounces, and lived for twenty-three hours. It seemed in that short time he had undergone every operation and had been on every machine possible. Mathew, Nathan's identical twin brother, was stillborn. He weighed two pounds. The birth and death of our first children happened within a very short period of time—twenty-four hours.

My husband, Warren, and I experienced so many feelings. We were shocked, angered, and isolated; there was utter despair and disbelief; and there was so much guilt and loneliness. The cards, letters, and visits were nice, but nothing helped, no one understood, except people who had gone through the same type of loss, the same type of anguish.

We had so many things we wanted to talk about, but almost no one wanted to listen (including our immediate families). We wanted to talk about details, like who the boys had looked like, the funeral, and the pregnancy. Yet everyone would tell us just "to forget about it, don't dwell on it."

No one wanted to listen except the parents of children who had died. No answers came for the question why. So many if onlys were gone over and over, and the guilt was horrible. Warren could not even understand some of the guilt feelings I was having about the boys' early birth, or many of the inadequate feelings I was experiencing. Through everything there was the question, "Why did our boys have to die? And "What are we supposed to be learning because they did die?"

Nicole was born 22 July, 1977, seven to eight weeks early. I had been in bed for about a month before she was born trying to stop another premature birth. It gave me plenty of time to wonder again about why me, and ask God what He wanted from me. What did all of this mean?

Nicole weighed four pounds, and looked almost big compared to her two brothers who had been born less than ten months earlier. She was in the hospital for about a month. The days passed, but very slowly. They were full of hope, worry, questions, and prayer. When she finally came home, weighing a huge four-and-a-half pounds, we were still a little scared of her and overprotective.

I felt like I would go crazy if anything happened to her, and I wondered if anyone else ever felt that way, if anyone else felt inadequate as a mother, if anyone else would like to hide her baby away from everyone to avoid any sickness? I felt like I had to do something or I would go crazy. I went back to school in January 1978 to begin working toward my master's degree in human development and family studies. I was still searching for something.

My advisor enrolled me in a class entitled Parent Education. Students were to form teams and recruit parents for a type of parent-group sharing, interaction, and education. I decided to get together a group of parents who had lost children to share concerns and just talk. My instructor approved and endorsed the idea and offered many suggestions and much needed encouragement. He was excited about the idea and felt it was a worthwhile cause. He did much to keep me going. My first goal in organizing this group was to locate parents who had lost children and who would be interested in this type of group. Names came from hospital personnel, church associates, and the community at large (including the university, staff, and students). From this my husband and I compiled a list of about a dozen couples. The next step was to contact them.

I was able to contact eight of these couples. Of these, four couples agreed to attend at least three meetings. I was honest with them, telling them I had organized this group to meet class requirements but also to meet a personal need. I also expressed a hope that maybe we would continue the group and eventually be of some service to the community.

The group of people was very diverse. There was a commonality, however: the death of an infant. The key to their attending was their own motivation, and desire to share, and their common background of loss. There also was a common goal expressed by all: to have someone to listen, understand, share experiences with, and maybe, eventually, to help others who experience the same type of tragedy. We had four couples then, who said they would be willing and even eager to attend.

Warren and I then set up some meeting times and started to begin organizing a type of outline. When talking with couples, we had determined some common interest areas and from these we made up the following outline:

Goals of Meetings

1. To bring together parents who have lost children at birth or within a short time thereafter;
2. To allow for the members of the group to share their experiences with the others in the group;
3. To combine experiences and input that could be of assistance to others who would be faced with this tragedy. This could be accomplished through a variety of different ways:
    a. forming a core council of parents to be on call;
    b. developing pamphlets to be published and distributed to individuals in the helping professions and to parents who lose children;
    c. writing an article that others could identify with;
    d. continuing small group meetings for support and encouragement.

Meeting Schedule

Meeting 1
A. Introduction of
    1. Jan and Warren Stork,
    2. Individual parents,
    3. Grief Center personnel.
B. Parents sharing personal grief experiences.
C. Discussion of what the group would like to see done.

Meeting 2
A. Introduction of hospital personnel
B. Discussion of hospital procedures and policies.
C. Free discussion.

Meeting 3
A. Information on funerals and autopsies.
B. Film *To Be Continued.*
C. Discussion on "Coping and How Life Has Changed."
D. Decision on group continuation.
E. Group ideas and suggestions.

Warren and I drew up this outline but did not expect to stick with it all the way; it did give us some structure and certainly lessened our anxiety.

The meetings were to begin in a structured manner; although that is not what happened.

The Grief Center representative was a suggestion of the professor's. I had been scared and nervous about getting the group started, and he suggested that I call the Grief Center. I did call because I needed support. The center had organized to "offer an opportunity for people who are experiencing grief to discuss their feelings and thoughts regarding the death of someone they love" (quote taken from the Grief Center pamphlet). The woman they referred me to had lost a small child and was very active in the Grief Center; she also taught a class on death and dying. When I talked to her she reassured me that when the group got together they would have plenty to talk about and that there was little danger of causing further suffering. She also volunteered to attend the first few meetings to be a back-up facilitator and if necessary, to keep things going. The meetings were set to begin.

Initial Meetings

Notes from the first three meetings are included here:

Meeting 1: April 4

The meeting began at 7:30 P.M. The last couple left around 11 P.M. There were eight in attendance (two husbands did not come). We drank lots of coffee and lemonade to relieve the initial tension and uneasiness.

The meeting began with introductions and a brief overview of the outline. We discussed what we, Warren and myself, expected from the group, our goals, and then we asked the group what they wanted. The common goal voiced was "to help ourselves and then to help others."

We then talked about our personal experience, allowing emotions to take over. Many said they were angry, lost, and disappointed. There was talk about the important others around us: how they didn't understand even though they repeatedly said they did; how they avoided talking about our child or children when that was exactly what we wanted to do. The misunderstandings, the hurt, and the crazy feelings were all gone over and shared. Everyone contributed, and everyone felt comfortable when speaking. Tears were shed and there was much laughter; there was emotion everywhere.

Our representative from the Grief Center shared with us that our group could be included in the Grief Center, though she wanted us to feel comfortable with our own feelings before we tried helping others.

My role as leader or facilitator seemed to be only important in the beginning to get things organized, to introduce people. Later I was no longer the one everything was addressed to; people just talked to everyone. It was great.

Analysis. At the first meeting, cohesiveness was apparent. People talked of their experience and trusted one another. We had the meeting in our living room with no interruptions. It was a comfortable place and the right size so that everyone could hear well and yet have plenty of body space. There was no one dominant talker, although of course, one or two people did do more talking than others. The leader's role was only apparent initially. Soon I, the leader, became one of the group. We sat in a circle formation so that everyone could see everyone else. I talked about my experience first and everyone eagerly modeled. One similar goal was voiced by all, and there was a high level of motivation. The norms that seemed to evolve were mutual respect, everyone got his or her chance to speak, and everything said was confidential.

Infant Crisis Parent League

Meeting 2: April 18

> Our numbers increased to twelve and we reintroduced everyone, trying to briefly fill all of us in on the others' experiences and losses. The hospital personnel were introduced and questions began at once as to policy and why the hospitals do things the way they do them, that is, asking immediately where the body is to be taken, having millions of forms to be signed before the parents even get some time alone, the nurse's education on death (if there is any). It turned out to be a very informative and emotional night for all. So many negative feelings were aired about hospitals and their cold aloofness.

Analysis. The closeness remained, even though four additional people were there. In fact, the group seemed even more close and intimate. Catharsis was evident all night. It was apparent that just to be able to air some of their dislike for hospital policy relieved some tension. Many things were said that had never been said before, not even to a spouse. It seemed better for self-understanding, and a better understanding of one's spouse was gained. My role as leader was minimal; the group as a whole was in control.

Meeting 3: April 25

> The same twelve people were in attendance again, and a real valuing of the group was evident. Everyone was comfortable and at ease and ready to talk. We began by talking about the week, how it had gone, what we had

thought about, our good days and our bad days and the stages of grief (Warren and I did do some teaching of specifics on the various emotions of grief). We then began a discussion and sharing about funerals, and the problems associated with funerals and autopsies. Again the meeting lasted over three hours. We all agreed we would like to continue meeting, and so another meeting time was set for the next month.

Analysis. My role as leader was more evident in this meeting, that is, teaching and facilitating discussion on funerals. The members responded well to this format, as though they wanted some relief from the draining emotional venting they had been doing more of in the other meetings. This group had definitely become cohesive and trusting. The goal of helping each other was being fulfilled, but now everyone wanted to do more.

Evolution of the Group

After the first three meetings the group had new goals. We wanted to get organized and help others. The experimental group then was split into a Sharing Group and a Task Group (organizing and establishing guidelines for becoming a helping group for others).

All summer and most of the fall was spent trying to decide what exactly we wanted our group to become. Half of the meeting would be devoted to sharing and supporting; the other half to task evaluation and problem solving. In the meantime, our community resources were growing. Many community groups wanted to know what we were doing and if they could be of any assistance. We also were becoming better known by talking to groups of student nurses and groups of students on campus about our experiences. So much was happening, and yet we still did not know what our exact focus or aim should be.

We had already increased group membership to twenty, although two couples were not always present. But cohesiveness did not seem to be a problem, even with the new additions and with the erratic attendance of a few. We still were well motivated and we allowed all new members to share their loss with us and we with them. By October, however, we decided not to enlarge our initial core group anymore. Rather, if others wanted to be included, we would break into two or three smaller groups.

During the summer, when we were still taking new members, a woman joined our group who had lost a baby to Sudden Infant Death Syndrome. She became part of our group because there was no group for her and she needed one. She became our resource person then on SIDS. She was soon the busiest, with referrals coming in often. At this time all referrals came through me, the leader. I would then try to assign a couple to follow up and report back to the group. We were not getting a lot of referrals; however, we did see a need for our type of group and our motivation remained high. By December we had decided on some specific goals to be implemented:

1. To remain active as a small support group or groups for sharing concerns and offering encouragement;
2. To provide hospital and home visits to parents of children who are very ill or premature and to parents whose infants have died (including SIDS);
3. To have several public informational meetings throughout the year on such topics as: the various emotions of grief; overprotection; and common infant crises;
4. To gather together a library of information and materials available to anyone in need.

We were meeting then at least once a month and also doing some calling on other parents on a one-to-one basis. By January we had made several calls on parents of children who were premature and on parents whose children had died. We got referrals through the Grief Center, pastors, hospital personnel, and other community organizations. The calls and visits we made consisted mainly of listening. We offered no medical advice, but did share some of our experiences and what had been helpful for us. Part two of our goal, to help others, was starting to be fulfilled.

In February we became an active, acknowledged volunteer group of St. Elizabeth's Hospital. We drew up a pamphlet and elected new officers: a chairperson, a program leader, and a referral secretary. We also approved and adopted a name for our group, the Infant Crisis Parent League. We are now actively engaged in in-service training sessions led by a psychologist in the group on what to do or not to do, what to say or not to say to a recently bereaved or traumatized parent. We are also organizing a series of community educational meetings; the first was on overprotection. We are seeing and talking with other parents who have lost children and making visits to the hospital. And last, but not least, we are still meeting to discuss our own needs and emotions.

The Infant Crisis Parent League is functioning well now. The organization has been designed and implemented. The motivation is high. Cohesiveness and a real valuing of the group is apparent. Norms have been established. We are becoming known in the community. But the best benefit is that this group does help the bereaved parent.

It has been great to talk about our children in an accepting environment, to cry where you feel safe and loved, to know someone understands, and to see others functioning again after such a terrible hurt and loss.

It is also a great feeling to help others; that is when we are really helping ourselves. We have learned through our own experiences that there many times are no answers, but it does help to have someone to cry with who can understand.

A Year Later

It has been almost three years now since our group first met, and, although the group is still functioning, things have continued to change and evolve. The core group, the really active people, are couples whose losses have been more recent. Warren and I still make a few calls, but our involvement has lessened. We still are very anxious to see that the group continues, and we certainly have not forgotten our sons, but other things have become more important. That is not only true of us, but also of the other couples who first began the group.

So many people tell you when your child dies that things will someday be okay. At that time you seriously doubt that you can ever feel happy and normal again. But it does happen; and it is a blessing and a relief that it does.

12 One Family's Story: Ellen and Bill

Ellen and Bill live in a pleasant, middle-class neighborhood in a well-kept house in the heartland of America. This is what happened to them after their baby Christopher died. We chose to include their in-depth story because they are among the many families who have survived SIDS, in spite of all the pain.

Ellen

Ellen was born in a very small town in the Midwest, a farming community of about fourteen hundred people. When asked about her early years, Ellen replied that what she remembers the most was that her father was the town drunk.

He was very successful when he first got married, Ellen reminisced. He owned a couple of farms and had a grocery store, and then he went through a variety of things: he was a mail carrier, a truck driver, and then he finally hit rock bottom and wasn't anything for about four years. Eventually he went through an alcohol treatment program at a hospital.

I was a junior in high school when he finally quit. And he did extremely well. He came home and started a rock-hauling business. Within about four years, he had an empire. Making incredible money and doing extremely well, a regular riches to rags to riches story.

I don't like to look back at it, really I don't. But if I had it to do over again, I would probably do it the same way because of what came out of it. The part of me that came out of it all has been helpful in later life. I think I have become a real survivor.

He didn't drink around the house, but he was always drunk. I didn't watch him pour the alcohol in his body, but he was sloppy, nasty drunk. We used to have to leave when he came home. My mom was smart enough to get us out of there. I can remember many nights that we drove around for hours, until she knew he had gone to sleep. Then we would go home and she would get up the next morning and go to work as a nurse. She did this throughout the entire thing. There was a period of time that I was very angry at her for allowing this to go on. I was angry at her for not getting out of the relationship. But she is an incredible lady, and I guess she knew—I don't know how. But she knew that it was all going to come out okay in the end. When I was growing up, it seemed like everybody else had a "normal" family. And I know now that they didn't. They just were faking it like everybody else.

It seemed like I was missing a real father figure. It was very humiliating to be down at the bowling alley with the crowd and watch your father go weaving back and forth down [the] main street. The kids were all cracking up.

But instead of letting it get the best of me and crawling into a shell, I didn't do that at all. I did tons of things in high school, and really put forth a lot of effort toward succeeding.

The most important thing about my experience is that it made me really understand that some people are very calloused toward alcoholics, calloused toward drug addicts, calloused toward all sorts of people with problems, basically because of ignorance.

I think having an alcoholic father has enabled me to understand and accept life experiences I may not be able to control. That experience during my childhood also has made me accept the fact that people often can be insensitive to what you may be experiencing, often because they really don't understand.

After a few years of college in California, I came back here and started working for a bank. The people who owned the bank thought that I was a promising person, so they sent me to St. Louis and put me through extensive training, and when I came back I went into management. I met Bill shortly after that. And my big career in banking went out the window. I worked while we were dating; we got married and I worked for about ten months after we got married.

The demands of my job did not really go well with being a bride, and really caring more about my marriage than the position, I decided to quit and devote more time to our marriage.

When Bill and I first got married we really didn't discuss having children. I really didn't feel I would ever be a mother, basically because I really had never been around children and I can honestly say they scared me to death. I had grown up an only child and had virtually no exposure to them. I liked children and felt they could bring great joy to a relationship, but then again they were frightening, and moreover, I was afraid of the great responsibility of raising a child.

There were many things that Bill and I did discuss when we first got married and one of those things was arguments. I have always felt strongly about never bringing up the past in an argument. It never seems to help to dredge up past wrongs; it only adds more hurt and anger to the problem you are dealing with at the time. This attitude I have can probably be attributed to my mother for she never held my father's past behavior over him during or after his drinking problem. I always admired her for this, and I really felt that is one of the reasons their marriage survived what it did.

Drinking was another thing Bill and I discussed. Bill likes to drink and let loose, but he doesn't make a habit of it. Bill knew from the beginning I wouldn't tolerate a drinking problem. I know I sound a little hypercritical, but I guess I felt if I laid down the law from the beginning maybe I would never have to deal with it later. Realistically, I'm really not sure how I would handle it. We are not the kind of people that have that ritual drink before dinner to relax, basically because I feel it can become a very dangerous habit. I feel very confident that neither one of us will ever have to deal with a drinking problem.

Another major problem we had to deal with before we got married was religion. Fortunately it did not become a major problem with us as it does for many people. I had been raised Catholic and Bill had been raised Lutheran. We both felt that one should not change for the other; we felt we should both make a sacrifice, so we became Methodist. This compromise was good for us, for that way we were both adopting something new together. By doing this neither one of us could feel like we sacrificed something for the other one.

We were married a little over a year when I got pregnant. We really hadn't discussed it much, but once I knew I was pregnant I felt very positive about it. I decided to do the best job I could at being a mother. I didn't read a lot of literature on parenting, and sometimes I'm not sure if that's a curse or a blessing. James, our first child, is not your ideal child, but I don't believe reading more would have helped. James is a really neat little kid, but he and I do have personality differences; we just don't mesh well. James and his father get along famously, and Bill read even less about child development than I did, so I'm not convinced some parents have more difficulty with a child than others do.

James was born two weeks early, and I was prepared to go over my due date so it was quite a surprise. Bill had been at a business meeting that night at which they had cocktails, and Bill had certainly had his share. When he finally arrived home I was furious with him; first of all for drinking, and second because I was unable to find him all evening. Bill decided not to respond to my anger and went to bed. He had no more gotten to bed and my water broke and off to the hospital we went. Bill was really very little help during the labor and I think he's still convinced he was in greater pain than I was. James was born after a long six-hour labor. The labor and delivery were difficult at the time, but now after having more children I feel the difficulty was merely not knowing what was going on or what was to be expected.

James was a beautiful baby and a very good one. I was quite scared of him at first, but somehow mother nature took over and I managed quite well.

Bill and I decided we wanted our children to be two years apart, so I became pregnant again, which ended in a miscarriage after about six weeks. Then I became pregnant again. I loved being pregnant, I always felt terrific and it was always a wonderful experience.

When James was born I had a fear of crib death. When the second baby Christopher was born, SIDS never entered my mind. I had had one beautiful baby that lived, so there was no reason for me to worry about this baby.

James was two and a half when Christopher was born. Chris was born the end of September. James never showed any jealousy toward Chris at all.

The labor and delivery of Christopher was very long, although after Chris decided to be born the delivery went very smoothly. He was a small baby when he was born, but he grew and progressed very normally.

He was an extremely good baby, an absolute angel. He never caused a problem at all, although he always got up for a four o'clock feeding at which he was quite delightful. There was something I noticed shortly before he died and that was that he seemed to have a lack of a startle reflex. I could slam a door right next to him, and he didn't seem to react at all.

He died in December. December twentieth. A week before Christmas. Upstairs. Two-and-one-half months old. Almost three months old. I wanted to move immediately.

I loved this house. I had worked my fool head off here. With all that work I had really kind of neglected Chris, and now this damned house has killed my baby.

The week that led up to Christopher's death has bothered me a little bit in that I was so busy getting ready for Christmas. I didn't spend as much time with him as I would have liked to. Fortunately, Bill's parents were here that week and Bill's mother just idealizes her grandchildren, and they really hadn't spent as much time with Chris as my parents had. Bill's mother took care of the boys most of that week as I was running errands, making drapes, and making Christmas cookies.

The next week on Wednesday—Chris died on Thursday—Bill was home all day as we were getting ready for Christmas, and we had a Christmas party to go to that night. I was in and out of the house all day and Bill was hanging the draperies I had made. Christopher wouldn't go to sleep, he was very content to sit in his infant seat and watch his father work and his big brother play. He never did take a nap that afternoon.

I tried to rock him to sleep. At one point he laid there and smiled at me and was so happy, and I figured, "Well, this is ridiculous. Face it, the kid is not tired." He got a little fussy when I was getting ready to go to the party that night, so I just took him from room to room where I was getting ready, and as long as he could see me he was all right. We left him with the baby-sitter and we went to the party.

It was very strange that evening; much of the conversation revolved around our children, particularly Christopher and what a delightful and good baby he was. Most of our friends at the time didn't have any children, and so we rarely talked about our kids. But that night was different. When we came home that night I did something I had never done before and that was I took the babysitter into Christopher's room to check on him. He had the sniffles, nothing serious, but we went in and checked on him and he was just fine. This was about 1 A.M. I took the baby-sitter home and she knew that he was fine when she left.

We woke up at eight o'clock, and I couldn't believe that he hadn't gotten up for his two o'clock feeding. He was finally sleeping through the night, I thought. He hadn't napped that whole day before, so I figured he was just so tired.

Then Bill went in to check on Christopher, and the first thing he hollared out was that "My God, he is gone." I thought somebody had taken him. That thought got planted in my mind, and I had nightmares for months afterward that somebody was going to kidnap James.

But then Bill said Chris was dead. I dialed 911, and I said, "Our baby is dead."

And the operator said, "Do you know mouth-to-mouth resuscitation?"

I thought to myself, "You dumb idiot, I just told you my baby is dead." But I said, "Yes, I know mouth-to-mouth resuscitation."

He said, "Can you apply it?"

I said, "It isn't going to do any good. My baby is dead."

"My baby is dead. My God, my baby is dead." There are no words to really explain the horror I felt, the anger, the confusion. I gave the rest of the information to the operator and hung up the phone. The fireman arrived within minutes of our phone call.

James had woken up and was sitting on the steps crying and didn't know what was going on. Bill would not let me go in the bedroom to see, and I didn't because of the fear of what I might see. I then came down the steps. I said to the fireman, "You have got to do something with James."

He said, "Can we take him next door?"

And I told him to take him next door to the Svoboda's and he did. The fireman picked Jim up and carried him over there. I didn't know where Bill was, so I went back upstairs and I did see Christopher. I am very glad that I did see him for Bill's sake.

It is not a pretty sight. But I was glad that I at least saw him because Bill would have alone had that vision forever and I would have never known that pain. Bill would have always known. He would have been the sole person who would have seen that horrible sight of our baby discolored and deformed.

I don't know if I could have stood it alone. This way we can share that awful feeling, and I can say, "I understand, I know what you saw and I know how awful it is." Had he had to cope with that by himself, I think it would have been hard. It would not only have been hard on him, but it would have been hard on me because I would have never known what he saw. It was awful—it was awful.

I went upstairs and the fireman had him. I never really held him, and I regret that terribly that I never really held him. The fireman had him, and I put my arms around the fireman and I just collapsed on the fireman holding Christopher. And when that happened there was a push of air out of Christopher. I looked at the fireman, and the fireman started to work on Christopher again. And then he explained to me that having both bodies push against Christopher worked some air out. That was the last time I ever saw him looking that way. And then they wrapped him in a white blanket. I then came downstairs and there was a nurse from the Mobile Heart Team.

She knelt by me and cried with me. And told me over and over again how it wasn't my fault and how there wasn't anything we could have done. She was the one who really got me headed in the right direction. Just the fact that she sat there. How can you say thank you for crying? But I did.

Our doctor arrived about an hour later to pronounce the body dead, and at this time he requested that we have an autopsy done. We had been told that it was SIDS, but he felt for our own well-being and for research it would be helpful. At first I was very resentful; I felt as if he were accusing me of something. We did decide to have the autopsy done, and I'm grateful that we did. The autopsy relieved any questions I had about the fact that it really was SIDS.

That day was a busy blur. With friends and relatives arriving I remember very little of the details. The one thing I remember vividly was that I was never going to have another child. I was never going to be put through this again.

Bill seemed to accept Chris's death so easily, at the time, and this angered me. Bill has always had a stronger faith in God, and I believe this was the reason he took it better.

The next day the mortuary called and told us Christopher's body was ready for viewing. Viewing dead bodies has always bothered me, but I so desperately needed to see Christopher. When I saw Chris lying there for the first time it really sunk in. He was dead. That horrible sight that we had found had been wiped away, and he lay there so angelic and peaceful. It was very comforting to see him that way.

We got through the funeral and the next few days quite well as we were surrounded by friends and relatives. Christmas came and went and all I can really remember was such emptiness. Then they were all gone and we were alone.

Bill and I had started a pattern of Bill always putting James to bed and I would put Christopher to bed. Bill took care of James at the table and I took care of Christopher. All of a sudden I had nothing to do. I had been robbed of my baby. So many times I thought, "Why me? Why my baby?" I would look at James sometimes and actually hate him. He constantly rejected me and wouldn't allow me to do anything for him. I thought to myself, "I hurt so badly how can you do this to me?"

Bill and I had a number of arguments about James. He felt I was short-tempered with James and that I wasn't very understanding of his needs. Bill felt what had happened really had effected James much more than we understood. In a way I was resentful, because I kept thinking, "This thing has effected me, too!"

Bill and I never pulled away from each other emotionally or sexually. If we ever needed each other, it was at this time. Often when married couples experience a crisis they pull away from each other in every way, but for Bill and me it was different. We seemed to come closer together.

I was convinced in the beginning that I could never have another baby, although the day of the funeral I remember standing in our bedroom getting ready and saying a silent prayer to myself. I was asking God to help me get through the day, and then I realized that our life as a family had to go on and having another baby was part of that going on. I strongly believed God wouldn't put me through this again, and if He did I would have to deal with it. I didn't make a decision then to have another baby immediately, but I really didn't fear getting pregnant.

Two months after Chris died I found out I was pregnant. I'm not sure when I got pregnant but it had to be within days of Chris's death. I wasn't trying to replace Christopher but I knew I wanted to have more children. I just wasn't sure if I was emotionally ready.

I didn't realize what the birth of Benjamin really did for all of us until a few months after he was born. There was fear, incredible fear, but along with that fear came a great healing process. Much of my anger was leaving me and to be able to love and be loved by another human being was wonderful. I was once again feeling good about myself and my life.

By the end of the pregnancy, I didn't think that this baby was going to solve any problems at all. I felt that maybe there were going to be a whole lot of problems. I thought I really was going to become a mental case; that it was going to be constant worry. I wasn't going to be able to sleep; I was going to make this baby crazy with overprotection.

Benjamin is without a doubt a very special child. I don't love him any more than James, but when I look at Ben I remember all the pain he managed to wipe away.

I worried more about Jim after the baby died. I still go in. I will go in often in the evening and just sit and look at him. Not so much just to check that he is still breathing, but just to sit and look and be thankful that we have gotten him to five years old. Maybe everybody sits and looks at their children and appreciates the fact that they are alive. But I don't think so. I think a parent that lost a child has a tendency to cherish those moments. My heart sinks a little bit every time James gets hurt.

Bill and I have always had good communication between us, and about a year ago I found we were being short-tempered with each other so we decided to make a pact to be nicer and more considerate of each other's feelings. We both realized that we were wasting such precious time in nagging each other, and you never know how much of that time you have left. When a family experiences a loss you become very aware of how impermanent things are.

After Benjamin was born, my cousin, who is a general practioner, urged us to have Ben monitored. Our family doctor didn't encourage us either way. I strongly felt that if we were going to lose Ben there was nothing we could do about it. I still believe that way, although I understand monitoring much better now and I see how beneficial it can be in many cases.

Bill and I have a strong belief in God and have accepted Chris's death and feel that that was the way it was to be. Many people don't feel that way, and I think it may change their way of handling it. I do believe that the faith we both share has helped us deal with the guilt that often accompanies parents after the loss of a child to SIDS.

I always feel somewhat more fortunate that my child died of SIDS than the mother who lost her child to a disease. My baby was apparently healthy; the autopsy reported that there was no apparent cause of death. Knowing that helps to erase some of the guilt. I feel confident that I took the best care I could of Christopher. In a sense we parents who lose children to SIDS are taken off the hook. There is still guilt, but at least there aren't those what ifs that often go along with losing a child to some sort of disease.

After Christopher died, someone said something to me about my smoking while I was pregnant. I felt so guilty and at the same time I wanted to wring her neck. I spoke to my doctor at length about my smoking and he was wonderful. He encouraged me to cut down my smoking, but he assured me that the smoking was not the reason Christopher died. He knew that I was not emotionally able right then to quit, so he didn't urge it.

The pregnancy was hard emotionally. But there were some light moments. We were on our way out to Rockford and the sun was setting. It was a glorious sunset. As we were driving out, we were heading west. It was that time of the evening where you could literally see the sun going down.

We are visiting and all of a sudden Jim pops up in the back seat and he says, "How does Christopher stay up there?"

And I said, "What do you mean?"

"Well," he said, "the sun is coming down, how does Christopher stay up in heaven with God?"

And I looked at Bill and we both looked at each other and we thought, "Gee, what do you say?"

Bill replied, "Well he has a chair up there to sit on." [Laughs.] I was waiting for this profound statement to come out of Bill and that was it. Jim never asked another thing. The sillyness—it's something you've just got to have to stay alive.

We had a horrible time the Christmas before Ben was born. I thought I was going to lose my mind. James just began to behave horribly. In the back of my mind I thought maybe.

Ben was the same age as Chris was, and it was the same time of the year. I was afraid that James was having fears of Ben possibly dying. Maybe this was the reason he was behaving so badly. I didn't want to bring up the subject. I feared if that wasn't the reason for his bad behavior, I didn't want to plant a fear there that wasn't there already.

Down deep I was afraid of the same thing. It seemed like I was sitting on a time bomb. One morning about a week before Christmas, James crawled into bed with me and said, "Mom, when is Ben going to die?"

And I said, "Well, Honey, we hope that he won't die." I knew that I couldn't say he is not going to die because I thought, "As soon as I say that, I'm going to get caught in one big mess." And I talked about it and said, "We hope that babies don't die, but sometimes they do."

And he said, "Well it is Christmas Mom, and Chris died at Christmas." He said, "Mom, all babies die," because all his babies had died.

The only baby that he had was Christopher, and he had died. We got another baby and he was going to die, too. So then I talked about different babies that we knew that didn't die and grew up. We had a little girl next door that was a baby about the same age as Christopher and she was almost two.

James seemed to accept the explanation, and we got through Christmas pretty well. Bill and I both cried after Christmas was over. We cried because we had gotten over another mountain in our lives.

Everyone told us that James would never remember the death of Christopher. He's only two and a half and he will forget. James didn't forget; he never will. Maybe if Christopher had died in the hospital it wouldn't have affected him so deeply, but going through the trauma that day with both of his parents half crazy with fear and bewilderment has really stuck with him.

He has fond memories of Chris and often mentions him. Small children don't know how to release their grief, and so James never cried. But he just seemed to ask endless questions. James finally was able to mourn when he was five years old. He and I took a bouquet of flowers to Chris's grave on Chris's birthday. When we got there James started to ask me some questions about Chris, and then all of a sudden he began to cry. He sobbed hysterically, begging me to get Chris back and all the time asking why. I held him and loved him and allowed him to get it all out. Together we sat and talked for nearly an hour at Chris's grave, sharing our feelings. And ever since that day I believe James has a better understanding of what really happened.

After Christopher died, in the first few days I started to withdraw badly. I was scared. I started to withdraw and it started to scare me because I usually don't back away from situations, I usually go full speed into them. I didn't want to talk and I didn't want to be talked to. I was feeling very sorry for myself. I was the only person this could happen to. Bill seemed to bounce back so quickly, I was a little angry. I thought, "What in the hell?" I wasn't talking. People were asking me questions and I wasn't answering them in the car on the way back from the funeral home. I could tell it was getting to Bill, but at this point I didn't care.

We got home and we got the phone call shortly afterward. At that time, I still didn't know for sure if it was SIDS. We had been told it was, but I thought, "God, I wonder if he got bumped. Maybe the baby-sitter dropped him and she didn't tell me, and he bled to death." A million things went through my head. Then when I got the autopsy report—Dr. Fritsch has a way of calming you—he said, "There was nothing you could have done, Ellen." He said, "The autopsy shows he was in very good health; he was just a normal baby." And it was like the whole world lifted off my shoulders. I hadn't done anything wrong. Thank God, I hadn't done anything wrong. And so then I got to feeling better.

I have never backed away from anything, and I felt this crisis in my life wasn't any different. I had to go on. Not only for Bill, James, and the baby I was caring for, but mostly for myself. It wasn't easy, and I didn't do it alone. Bill was truly my strength, and all our wonderful friends and family were so good, too. They all listened, and they never seemed to say the wrong thing. I have worked with SIDS families who have had someone say something hurtful and stupid to them. That makes it all the more difficult to heal. Maybe somebody did say something to me that could have been taken the wrong way. Maybe, but I just didn't hear them or I didn't want to hear it.

Now when I think of Christopher, I think, I have lost him for now, but I know I will find him again. The word dead is very final.

In my mind that means he is gone forever and that is not the way we look at it. He is still very much a part of our family, very much a part of our life. I feel we have three children, unfortunately one of them isn't with us.

I don't ever want to forget him, and we never will. There are things that still hurt, and times that are very hard. When I hear ''Away in a Manger'' played it always tears me apart. But it's not bad to cry. It's not bad to be human.

Bill

I was born in Chicago and I lived there until about third grade and then we moved to Springfield. I graduated from high school in Springfield and was in chemistry for three years at the University of Illinois before switching to business. After graduation I went to work for a small industry, and I'm a manager now.

I met Ellen through her cousin. We weren't too crazy about each other at first, but I needed a date for a fraternity function and I couldn't find anyone so I called her. Nine months later we were married. It was a real whirlwind romance. We had good communication after we decided to like each other. I really don't know what happened. We could talk and we didn't have any problems.

After about a year Ellen got pregnant and our first son James was born. Two years later Christopher was born.

I don't really like little babies. They have got to grow a little bit. I don't feel right handling five-pound creatures. They just have got to grow a little bit before I feel comfortable. I feel like I'll break them. Christopher was about three months old when it happened. We had been to a Christmas party that night.

The funny thing about this is that I hadn't had very much to drink that night at the Christmas party. I came home and I drank some coffee and I was not tired at two in the morning, so I stayed up until all the television shows were off at 3:30, drinking milk and eating cookies. Ellen was sound asleep. I was up until after 3:30 when I went to bed, and to the best of my knowledge, Chris was dead at that time. It was at or around the time he died that I went to bed. There was no sound and we had the doors wide open.

The next morning he slept late, and I went in and checked on him and thought, ''Somebody has stolen him.'' He wasn't lying there in his crib. I saw his blankets over in the corner. He was under them. I picked him up. I knew he was dead. I didn't know what to do. I was panicked.

I tried to keep Ellen out of the room. I didn't want her to see him, because he was pretty well—he looked bad. I got very loud. I was angry. I was yelling at her to stay in our room and I was over in the baby's bedroom with Christopher. I just didn't want her to see him because when I took the blankets off him his mouth was distorted and his eyes were open. I didn't want Ellen to see him like that. I knew he was dead.

I am talking slowly about it now, but as it was going through my head, it was unbearable. Do I call the morgue or do I—Who do I call? I put the baby on the bed, on the other bed. And then, by this time James was awake and crying on the steps.

I yelled at Ellen, "I don't want you to—don't come in here—stay out!" And she was handling the phone so she stayed out, and to be honest with you I don't know if she went in or not because she called 911 and I thought I had better get some clothes on: "Someone will be here." I laid him down, then I had him covered up, and I went in and put on a pair of jeans. I came back out of the bedroom and a fireman was standing at the front of the door. They were here immediately.

I couldn't believe it. If there had been any chance, we would have saved him. That fireman took him and worked with him in the bathroom and he tried everything. I can't blame anybody.

The fire department came, they were the first. The Heart Team was here and then the sheriff. Then the coroner. The fireman closed his eyes. I didn't want Ellen to see the baby and yet—I can understand the mother not really wanting to touch the child, but wanting to touch to see if it is true. To realize the baby is dead.

Seeing him in the casket helped. Ellen had always said that she had never wanted to ever have an open casket. She changed her mind after we lost our baby.

I have my memories now of Christopher the way I want to remember him. I think that maybe in our case it was extremely relieving. It helped to soften that earlier ugly memory. He looked very angelic and just to have his face back in an undistorted manner was so relieving.

When I found him he appeared to be in such pain, even though everyone said it was a painless death. It's good to be able to remember him the way he was in the casket, at peace, his face natural and calm.

The day that Christopher died, it fell to me to talk to Jim. That night when he asked Ellen about what happened to Christopher, she froze right there and she gave me a look that signaled help: "I can't tell him," her eyes said. Nothing would come out of her mouth. So I took Jim upstairs and talked to him.

I took him into Christopher's room. The big one. It had a bed in there and a crib. I took him into Christopher's room—what came about is that Jim had moseyed upstairs and he went into Christopher's room and for the first time realized the firemen were not going to bring Christopher back, and Christopher wasn't in the crib.

He started asking the questions: "When are they finally going to bring him back?" He just thought that the fireman had him for a little visit. So I just sat him down and tried to explain it to him. Christopher went to heaven and God had chosen him and wanted him to be with God. And it would be sad for us, but Chris was very fortunate. And Jim said, "Well, when is God going to bring him back?" This is when I told him Christopher wouldn't be coming back. I thought he did an excellent job of comprehending.

The next morning was worse. We went to Christmas Eve services, and I didn't want to take him in at first; but neither one of us really thought what was going to come would come. We were sitting in the pew and he said, "Well, we gonna see Christopher tonight?"

I said, "He is with God."

"We are here, where is he?" He knew the church was God, and you know, we are here. What was the deal?

Telling anyone was a problem. The day Chris died, I called my best friend Fred, and then I thought I would call my folks and let them know. That didn't work, because I called Fred to tell him and that took me five minutes to get out of my mouth what I was trying to say. And I thought, "If I can't call my best friend there is no way I am going to call my parents."

When I called Fred I just tried to say, "He is dead." The word dead is very hard to say. I started to say it. I just kind of choked up, and I couldn't get it out in one nice sentence, what had happened to Christopher.

Fred finally asked, "Has something happened to Christopher?"

And I said "Yes." "He is gone." I could get "gone" out.

Then he knew what I meant. He said, "Do you want us to come over right now?"

And I said, "I would really appreciate it."

The hard part for the next few days was the planning. The fellow at the funeral home, he said to us many times, "This is very difficult. It is very difficult for me, I had a grandson just exactly the age of the baby, your baby, that died. And I've got to be honest with you, this is hard for me." He had seen death thousands and thousands of times, and it was hard on him.

I talked to the people at the funeral home afterward and thanked them for the very professional job. They did an excellent job. They were fantastic. They were very professional. The bill was very inexpensive. I just couldn't believe it. When I asked them about it they said that is just their policy and the way I got it, it is kind of a common thing in the whole industry. They just figure the last thing you need is a financial burden. They feel that the death of a young child is a trauma for everybody involved. And they don't want to make it harder for you if they can. That is the way they do it. I questioned it because I thought they had forgotten something on the bill.

One of the hard things besides finding him, I had a hard time at the mortuary that night. The next hardest thing was at the funeral. We were sitting in the limousine and people were filing out of the church and I saw six guys from my National Guard group in their uniforms. They had come, and they had come in a hell of a snow storm, and it was kind of—there were lots of friends there, that we knew would be there, but these were people who I had commanded. They knew us, but they didn't know us real well. It wasn't a thing where they had to be there. It was a very genuine act for them to do this and to be there in full uniform. It meant a lot to me.

I didn't feel like I was being strong for others. But in a sense I was strong. I think a lot all gets back to the achievement aspect of what you think of yourself and what you want to contend with. A lot of it came from my military background. I have had to tell men how to face death, what death is, and I can't tell them if they believe in God that is the answer. But I can't tell them that door isn't open either. I can't say, "Okay, if you believe in God you can face death. If we go into battle and your buddy gets killed, if you believe in God, you will make it right on through on trust." I can't say that because half of them don't believe in God. That is why it is hard for me to tell you my beliefs because going through the stages we do to try to prepare men for war—whether we ever see war or not—we still have to teach them. But after you get done talking about death, there is still the one thing that always comes up in the military and that is the mission. And to accomplish the mission. Whether it be at all cost. My belief was to do that at as small a cost as possible. But still the fact remains that in the indoctrination that I had to administer, the mission was always number one. And you know, after you preach that for so many years, and then it happens to you, you are faced with death, when I wanted to break down, I never could. I preached it for too damn long to turn around—I had to be strong.

In the initial few days, I wanted to go out and knock down garages with a sledge hammer. I wanted to fly off in a rage. And I couldn't because of the state Ellen was in. That was true and was the only time that I ever felt that I just had to stay together and that was all there was to it.

I feel I have been allowed to mourn all I wanted. I don't feel that I have been restricted at all. We communicate, Ellen and I. I can let a lof of grief out just by talking. Maybe it is relaxing for me to talk with Ellen, I don't know. But that is one way I can express my grief.

I have met people who can't talk at all. They just can't let anybody know anything. And how they would get across then that feeling I had inside the first day or what they could do with their grief, I just don't know.

They have got to do something. They have got to let it out somewhere, some way. Each marriage, you know each other, and you know when to let each other be strong or weak.

I would say on this particular subject, the death of Christopher, I was stronger because I had less feelings toward the baby than she had. They were so much closer; in my mind I had to be strong, in this particular instance.

It is a hell of a lot easier to be strong if there is someone who is strong with you. We share power. There is no struggle.

You can never erase a mistake, but you can sure offset it with achievements. And so, consequently, it is the same way with death. You might have a wound over here, but all the good things that happen are building up together on the other side of the fence. It never goes away. No way does it go away, but these good things over here continue to grow and pretty soon your scale is going to weigh out. Still, thirty years down the road, Christmas is going to be hard.

When we chose the music for the funeral, we had "Away in a Manger" played. Thirty years from now that song is still going to effect me in the same way it does now. I think the only other thing that is never going to change in thirty years, is that I will never forget the way he looked when I found him. No way. What I did all day that Thursday and Friday in thirty years is probably going to be forgotten. But the way he looked will never pass.

Little things bring back memories. Like I went to a funeral that was for an older person that had passed away, he was a vet. And there was a color guard right there. These guys never did any ceremony when Chris died, but they were in uniform. Anytime I go to a funeral and see a uniform, it is going to get me. Just little things. They are always going to be there, and they are always going to come back. When they reoccur, when you see them, you think about it all over again.

It is hard to know what you will remember, but that night at the mortuary I remember feeling that I was looking at Christopher for the first time. I realized for the first time that Christopher would never get to what I call a father stage, like James had. "I am never going to get a chance for that kid to get to me." He had already got into the mother stage. Ellen could feel a loss I wasn't really part of. I didn't know that before I actually saw him there in the casket and realized that I am never going to get that experience.

My son Jim has his own tools. They are not play tools, they are a real-life hammer and saw. And every time I do projects, he is right there with me, he takes them along. It gives him something to do. He nails nails and saws boards. I enjoy having him there. The kid is good. I'd just as soon have him doing that as anyone. It is great.

Christopher never got to that stage, of course, since at three months he died. That afternoon I was hanging curtains, the little guy wouldn't go to sleep, so I had him right there, and I would give him a toy hammer and he was chewing on it or something. But he was awake and with me. It was the only time that I had ever spent any real time with him because he had never got to that stage. When I saw him in the casket, that is when it hit me, what I really lost.

We had pictures taken at the funeral, which may seem morbid. But after we talked about it in my mind I kind of wanted the photographers there so that I could get the picture of him when I found him out of my mind. It keeps recurring and I have to have something to go back to and remember. Something that is tangible that I can look at. I am looking at two memories and one is horrible. One is more impressed on my mind—the one where I found him, not the one of seeing him in the casket. I got to thinking, ''I know which one is more likely going to stick in my mind the longer. I would like not to have it there.'' So we have the funeral pictures. If I didn't, then I lose that memory and that would be awful.

We don't want to lose him. You don't ever want to lose him. They are just so much a part of you. To put that baby away forever would be awful. He wasn't here that long, but he was here. He existed. And it is just like trying to erase, you just can't erase part of your past. It happened. Just try to take something out of it and try to put it into your life and make something out of it. Mold it into a positive experience. There is something there you can get out of it.

When I think of my family, we are still missing one. One is missing. And we feel that. There should be one in the middle. You know, a two-year old.

It's funny. Ellen has a cousin who has three boys. The oldest is kind of artsy, a very sensitive person, very strong willed. The middle one, he could care less. He is a hard worker, quiet, but he could care less about win or lose. Not competitive at all, a big mediator. The third one is rather ornery and he keeps trucking right on down the line. The middle one keeps peace in the whole household. It is just kind of funny; Ben will be getting kind of ornery, and Jim and Ben go at it. I say to Ellen, ''You know we are missing that middle one to keep the peace around here.'' Christopher was very gentle and quiet. When you see that, you wonder, ''What could have been?''

A Year Later

Bill and Ellen are surviving quite well. Their relationship is strong and healthy, and their love for each other seems to be even greater than ever.

They both have gotten involved with a SIDS support group in their area and find it to be very rewarding. They are doing well, but they still have some difficult times. It is a struggle, and they both have agreed that there will always be difficult days, difficult times. But these days are farther apart, and the time is not so long. The struggle to heal never ends, but without the struggle they would not have survived. Life will never be the same for Bill and Ellen; it has become infinitely more precious.

13 Conclusion

To fall in love with a baby can be one of the most beautiful experiences in an individual's life. The structure and texture of this love is so different from the love that adults feel for each other. Many new parents wonder if they could truthfully say they had ever known what love was before. For perhaps the first time they experience an unselfish, unlimited love, and they rejoice when they find it is an experience that is repeated with succeeding births. The definition and boundaries of love previously held widen and deepen as it is perceived that love and the capacity to love is limitless.

Tragically, the parents who contributed to this book and thousands of others find themselves confronted with a situation that forces them to discover the existence of the other end of the spectrum of emotion: the truth that pain is also limitless. They once wondered in awe, "How can I feel so much love?" Now their world is turned upside down and they cry, "I hurt so much, I can't hurt any more." A new day dawns, and they find that sorrow is bottomless.

A baby dies and the grief that grips these individuals is so intense that nothing could have prepared them for the nightmare they find themselves in. But the sun does continue to come up. Again and again. And just as they think they are healing, a slight jar again tears the scab off the wound and they wonder once more, "How long will it hurt?"

Every day can be an eternity of reliving brief moments of their baby's life. The world appears in sharp relief; as those outside the circle of grief offer the symbols of comfort they are studied carefully as every nuance of conversation is searched for implications of guilt.

Was it my fault? Did I do something wrong? Did I kill my baby? Magical thinking does not end with childhood. Although as adults we have put aside Santa Claus and the Tooth Fairy, retribution for bad thoughts stays with us. How could I have ever resented him for waking me up at two A.M.? Am I being punished for having such bad thoughts? Questions, more questions, self-doubt, guilt, and pain fill the void left by death.

Sitting in a living room with parents who have lost a baby, our pain is so intense that self-protection tells us to leave quickly. But we stay, forcing our eyes away from an oil portrait of the infant, lovingly enshrined with tiny ceramic angels. Our pain is almost overwhelming, but as we sit drinking coffee, smoking endless cigarettes, crying, our questions pervade: "How have they survived?" "How are they able to relive once more the death of their baby?"

The events of that day or that night the baby died stand out with a fresh clarity for these parents that time will not dull. To be told, "Don't think about it, it'll only make you sad," is incomprehensible. Oh, that they wouldn't have to think about it! But it creeps in unasked for, a pervasive fog, claustrophobic at times, somewhat manageable at others.

One father told us:

> I would wake up in the morning and think about getting the bottle warmed before she woke up. And then it would hit me: she's dead. I hated myself for the times I had lain in bed wishing I didn't have to get up. If I could just push it all away, and go back to those few minutes of peace before I remember it all. I wanted to hold on to those precious seconds of sanity when everything was okay, before it all happened, before I remember. But I always remember. I can't stop remembering.

In most of the popular press (and this book is no exception), in recounting the crisis of SIDS the high divorce rate among parents is cited. As a culture we might want to click our tongues with the thought, "Just when they needed each other the most." And some of us with not a little conceit privately may conclude that since they were failures as parents, it is not surprising that they are failures at marriage. But let us put aside our protective callousness for a moment, and consider that our children could die and that our marriage could also die. Then we can really appreciate the strength of these parents who face a crisis so extraordinary that nothing can prepare them for it. All around us marriages fail because two adult people seemingly cannot agree on who is to take out the garbage. So, it is truly amazing to us that any marriage can survive the death of a baby. Rather than censoring these people for a failed relationship, they should be afforded the highest praise for managing to remain intact, functioning individuals.

One fact that surfaced during the five years of our research was that these parents did not turn to suicide as a way out of the pain. We are not saying that suicide has not occurred after the death of a baby. This area deserves closer study. We have heard of but a single case. Where then did these parents find the strength?

For some, it was a deep faith in God; some were able to find strength from their marriage and family; and still others turned inward and called on resources they never new existed. For all of them it was as if the entire family had been in a terrible accident. Each of them emerged hurt in a different way, often without the ability to put into words how they were wounded. Sometimes this fact is incomprehensible to others within the family. Their own pain and grief causes their perspective to constrict. They then cannot understand the intensity of hurt anyone else might feel. One mother said: "I was an open, throbbing wound, and he wanted to have sex. It was very hard for me to understand that he was also in pain and that he felt our closeness would be healing. But how could he say that? He didn't know how to say it. It was something that he felt."

Contrary to popular cliches, it is not possible to share pain. If it were possible, these parents would have given it all away long ago. The death of a baby becomes a part of their lives and must be incorporated into a script entitled *The Great American Dream,* which for these parents has become a nightmare.

In this age of the battle of the sexes it has been pointed out by some that mothers are better prepared for the death of their children than fathers. Mothers, the argument goes, ready themselves for the worst every time they hear the screech of car tires in the street. Imagining blood and broken bones when a crash is heard is part of their lives, as well as wondering "Where are the children?" as an ambulance siren wails in the distance. Mothers do conjure up poisonings, accidents, and other assorted catastrophes, but not as any kind of preparation for death. Rather, these thoughts help to insure the rescue and continued survival of their children. Mothers and fathers know that if they are conscientious and careful, ever alert to danger, the children will be safe. We found no difference between men and women in this respect. They suffered equally and regained some level of adjustment at about the same time.

The course of life for parents who lose a baby to SIDS is altered forever. Gone are the illusions that they have some measure of control over their own lives. They slowly and painfully acquire new insight into the limits of their power. Never again are they able to believe that through the sheer intensity of their love will they be able to stay the harsh realities of life and death.

The courage and the resilience of these parents is truly remarkable. In their pain they discover new truths about themselves. Sometimes these truths are not always attractive, but a resolve begins to grow that life is worth living, and happiness is possible. The naive euphoria of parenthood is gone, never to be recaptured. But in its place there comes a new value to life: an appreciation for the fragility of our existence, coupled with a profound understanding that to live is also to experience death. To learn to live until we die is both the secret these parents share and the burden they shoulder.

**Appendix
Coping with Sudden
Infant Death:
A Self-Study Guide
for Parents**

Appendix
Coping with Sudden Infant Death:
A Self-Study Guide for Parents

As the reader has seen, the process of coping with SIDS is a long and complicated one. This appendix is comprised of a series of study questions that a parent can answer in writing or in his or her mind about how well he or she is doing in adapting to the crisis. We believe it could be very useful to reply to the questions in writing. A second questionnaire is also included; by filling it out a few months after filling out the first one, a person can see how much progress has been made. Coping with a crisis is like a child growing: unless you have a photograph or an aunt who does not come too often to tell you how fast your child is growing, you just do not see the changes.

Couples might find it helpful to fill out the questionnaire individually and then discuss how their responses are similar or how they differ. A discussion of these issues can go a long way toward easing the tensions and preventing misunderstandings. Remember, as Earl Grollman says, "Anything mentionable is manageable." If a couple cannot discuss these matters with each other, we suggest they do so with the aid of a professional counselor. A counselor working with SIDS parents would play the role of mediator and referee: making sure that each person understands the other, and that communication between people proceeds in a positive manner. (Counselors could have parents fill this questionnaire out before sessions, and follow up at the end of treatment by having them fill the questionnaire out again.)

The process of grieving moves along more quickly, we believe, if it is a shared experience with loved ones and friends.

Questionnaire 1

Date_____

Name (optional)_____

Address_____

1. Please write what you have gone through since your baby died.

2. What things have people done during this time that have been helpful to you? Have you told them so?

3. What things have people done during this time that have made it harder for you? Have you told them so, in a kind but firm manner?

4. What would you like people to know about how to treat a person who is grieving over a baby's death?

5. Who was caring for the baby at the time of the death?

6. Who found the baby?

7. What made this person look in on the baby?

8. What did she or he see?

9. How did this person react?

10. Whom did the person contact first?

11. Whom were you in contact with during the next few days (doctor, nurse, law officers, coroner, friends, relatives, and so forth?

12. Of all these people whom you were in contact with, who were the most helpful, and why?

13. Was an autopsy performed?

14. If so, did knowing the results and their explanation help?

15. When you first realized the baby was gone, what went through your mind as a probable cause of death?

16. Did you ever feel personal guilt over the death? If so, why?

17. Was it ever explained to you by anyone that in the case of Sudden Infant Death Syndrome no one can reasonably be held responsible for the death because medical science is not yet aware of its causes?

18. If you answered yes, was this explanation helpful?

19. Below is a list of events people describe as crises. Family crisis has been defined as a disruption in the routine operation of a family. Please check any that you have experienced in your lifetime. These may be personal experiences or experiences that have happened to others in your family that affected you. Give your age at the time of the crisis, and indicate how long the crisis lasted. (By length of time we mean how long did it take to resume normal activities, or reorganize your life to a satisfactory level.) Then circle the appropriate number to indicate the severity of the crisis.

Types of Family Crisis	Your Age at Time of Crisis (Years)	Length of Time (Years)	(Days)	Slight Crisis	Moderate Crisis	Extensive Crisis	Severe Crisis
_____ Hospitalization	_____ _____	_____ _____ /	_____ _____	1	2	3	4
_____ Loss of a child due to Sudden Infant Death	_____ _____	_____ _____ /	_____ _____	1	2	3	4
_____ Loss of a child by other causes	_____ _____	_____ _____ /	_____ _____	1	2	3	4
_____ Loss of a spouse	_____ _____	_____ _____ /	_____ _____	1	2	3	4
_____ Orphanhood	_____ _____	_____ _____ /	_____ _____	1	2	3	4
_____ Separation for military service	_____ _____	_____ _____ /	_____ _____	1	2	3	4
_____ Separation for work	_____ _____	_____ _____ /	_____ _____	1	2	3	4
_____ Alcoholism	_____ _____	_____ _____ /	_____ _____	1	2	3	4
_____ Crime	_____ _____	_____ _____ /	_____ _____	1	2	3	4
_____ Delinquency	_____ _____	_____ _____ /	_____ _____	1	2	3	4
_____ Drug addiction	_____ _____	_____ _____ /	_____ _____	1	2	3	4
_____ Marital unfaithfulness	_____ _____	_____ _____ /	_____ _____	1	2	3	4
_____ Nonsupport	_____ _____	_____ _____ /	_____ _____	1	2	3	4
_____ Progressive disagreement	_____ _____	_____ _____ /	_____ _____	1	2	3	4
_____ Adoption	_____ _____	_____ _____ /	_____ _____	1	2	3	4
_____ Birth	_____ _____	_____ _____ /	_____ _____	1	2	3	4
_____ Deserter returns	_____ _____	_____ _____ /	_____ _____	1	2	3	4
_____ Relative moves in	_____ _____	_____ _____ /	_____ _____	1	2	3	4
_____ Reunion after separation	_____ _____	_____ _____ /	_____ _____	1	2	3	4
_____ Step-parent marries in	_____ _____	_____ _____ /	_____ _____	1	2	3	4
_____ Annulment	_____ _____	_____ _____ /	_____ _____	1	2	3	4
_____ Desertion	_____ _____	_____ _____ /	_____ _____	1	2	3	4
_____ Divorce	_____ _____	_____ _____ /	_____ _____	1	2	3	4
_____ Illegitimacy	_____ _____	_____ _____ /	_____ _____	1	2	3	4
_____ Imprisonment	_____ _____	_____ _____ /	_____ _____	1	2	3	4
_____ Institutionalization	_____ _____	_____ _____ /	_____ _____	1	2	3	4
_____ Runaway	_____ _____	_____ _____ /	_____ _____	1	2	3	4
_____ Suicide	_____ _____	_____ _____ /	_____ _____	1	2	3	4
_____ Homicide	_____ _____	_____ _____ /	_____ _____	1	2	3	4
_____ Other, specify	_____ _____	_____ _____ /	_____ _____	1	2	3	4

20. Rank the crises you checked in order of severity.

21. What are the similarities and the differences between those previous crises in your life and the loss of your baby?

22. Did you or your spouse resume normal activities first after the death? Why?

23. Presumably, you and your spouse have different ways of coping with the death. What are they and why?

24. If you feel you need to talk with someone, whom do you turn to most often? Why?

25. Did you ever seriously consider a divorce from your spouse in the aftermath of the death? If so, why?

26. Did any family violence occur as a result of the death? What happened? Why?

27. Has drinking or drug use increased in the family because of the death? Whose? Why?

28. Did you ever just want to go to sleep and wake up after the pain is gone away? Why? When?

29. Have you ever thought of suicide? What are your arguments for it? Why shouldn't you?

30. What effect has the baby's death had on your religious faith?

31. Was your religious faith of any use to you in this crisis? How?

32. If you are a church member, did that institution support you? How?

33. Are there any other groups or organizations in your community that supported you in this crisis? How?

34. Has your relationship with other family members been affected by the death? How?

35. If you have other children, have there been any changes in the way you care for them?

36. Has the death affected your decision to have other children? How?

37. Did the other children attend the funeral? How did they react?

38. Did the children ask questions about the death? What did you reply?

39. Was there any difference in the children's behavior after the death (bed-wetting, nightmares, and so forth)?

40. Getting back to the overall problem of Sudden Infant Death, what else could have been done to help you in the crisis?

41. Have you done anything to help other people who have lost babies? What?

42. Does your community have a support group for grieving parents? Have you called them for help? Have you called them to offer your help?

43. We would like to try to get some idea how the Sudden Infant Death affected you personally. We would like to understand some of the feelings you experienced about yourself in relation to the death. Circle the appropriate number to describe your feelings for each time period.

	Very Unhappy	Somewhat Unhappy	Average	Somewhat Happy	Very Happy
1 year before the death, I was,	1	2	3	4	5
9 months before the death, I was	1	2	3	4	5
6 months before the death	1	2	3	4	5
3 months before the death	1	2	3	4	5
The death of the child	1	2	3	4	5
3 months after the death	1	2	3	4	5
6 months after the death	1	2	3	4	5
9 months after the death	1	2	3	4	5
1 year after the death	1	2	3	4	5
1 year 3 months after the death	1	2	3	4	5
1 year 6 months after the death	1	2	3	4	5
1 year 9 months after the death	1	2	3	4	5
2 years after the death	1	2	3	4	5
2 years 3 months after the death	1	2	3	4	5
2 years 6 months after the death	1	2	3	4	5
2 years 9 months after the death	1	2	3	4	5
3 years after the death	1	2	3	4	5

44. Now consider only the three-month period immediately after the death and circle the appropriate number to describe your personal feelings for each time period.

	Very Unhappy	Somewhat Unhappy	Average	Somewhat Happy	Very Happy
1 day after, I was	1	2	3	4	5
3 days after, I was	1	2	3	4	5
1 week after death	1	2	3	4	5
2 weeks after death	1	2	3	4	5
3 weeks after death	1	2	3	4	5
1 month after death	1	2	3	4	5
1 month 1 week after the death	1	2	3	4	5
1 month 2 weeks after the death	1	2	3	4	5
1 month 3 weeks after the death	1	2	3	4	5
2 months after the death	1	2	3	4	5
2 months 1 week after the death	1	2	3	4	5
2 months 2 weeks after the death	1	2	3	4	5
2 months 3 weeks after the death	1	2	3	4	5
3 months after the death	1	2	3	4	5

45. Now consider your family organization or integration in relation to the various time periods surrounding your child's death. (In other words, how smoothly the family was functioning as a whole.)

	Highly Disorga- nized	Somewhat Disorga- nized	Average Level of Organi- zation	Somewhat Well Orga- nized	Very Well Orga- nized
1 year before the death	1	2	3	4	5
9 months before the death	1	2	3	4	5
6 months before the death	1	2	3	4	5
3 months before the death	1	2	3	4	5
The death of the child	1	2	3	4	5
3 months after the death	1	2	3	4	5
6 months after the death	1	2	3	4	5
9 months after the death	1	2	3	4	5
1 year after the death	1	2	3	4	5
1 year 3 months after the death	1	2	3	4	5
1 year 6 months after the death	1	2	3	4	5
1 year 9 months after the death	1	2	3	4	5
2 years after the death	1	2	3	4	5
2 years 3 months after the death	1	2	3	4	5
2 years 6 months after the death	1	2	3	4	5
2 years 9 months after the death	1	2	3	4	5
3 years after the death	1	2	3	4	5

Questionnaire 2

Date_____

Name (optional)_____

Address_____

1. Let about three to six months pass after filling out questionnaire 1. Before you begin writing, carefully study what you wrote in the past. Now, write down all that has happened to you since that time.

2. What still hurts? When does it hurt? Why? What are you doing to alleviate your pain?

3. What good things have you learned about life?

4. What good things have you learned about yourself?

5. What will the future bring?

6. What are you going to do to help other people who have been to the edge?

Index

Index

About the Authors

John DeFrain received the Ph.D. in family studies from the University of Wisconsin, Madison. He is an associate professor in the Department of Human Development and the Family, University of Nebraska, Lincoln. Dr. DeFrain codirects a postgraduate program in marriage and family counseling, and is a coordinator of the National Symposium on Building Family Strengths. He teaches courses in marriage and family relationships, and his research, supported by the Agricultural Experiment Station at the University of Nebraska, Lincoln, focuses on families in crisis. He has coedited four books on family strengths and coauthored a dozen professional articles in various journals. His research has been reported in *Human Behavior, Psychology Today, Children Today, McCall's Working Mother, National PTA Today,* and *Ladies' Home Journal.* Findings from the SIDS research with Jacque Taylor and Linda Ernst have been reported in *Reader's Digest Families, Parents* magazine, and *Psychology Today.*

Jacque Taylor received the M.S. in human development and the family from the University of Nebraska, Lincoln. She is director of the Office on Domestic Violence in Riverton, Wyoming, which is currently active in setting up a shelter for battered women.

Linda Ernst received the M.S. in human development and the family from the University of Nebraska, Lincoln. She did doctoral work in family studies at Brigham Young University in Provo, Utah, and now is completing the Ph.D. at the University of Minnesota, St. Paul. She teaches courses in marriage and family relationships at the University of Minnesota, St. Paul, and St. Olaf College in Northfield, Minnesota.